Recipes of the Stars

Eating Like Hollywood Royalty

Over 100 Classic Recipes Spotlighting Many Favorite Celebrities

Also by Leo Pearlstein
Celebrity Stew

☆ ☆

Recipes of the Stars

All rights reserved. No part of this book may be reproduced or transmitted in any form or by any means, electronic or mechanical, including photocopying, recording or by any means of information storage and retrieval system without express written permission from the publisher, except in the case of brief quotations embodied in critical articles and reviews, permitted by copyright law. All inquiries should be addressed to:

HOLLYWOOD CIRCLE PRESS

P.O. Box 48051
Los Angeles, CA 90048
Website: www.celebritystew.com

This book is available through most bookstores or directly from the publisher at the above address or website.

Printed and bound in the United States of America

Recipes of the Stars
Copyright 2004 By Lee & Associates, Inc.
Library of Congress Control Number 2002112547
First Edition
ISBN 0-9711306-2-0

Design by Bill Goldfine, Los Angeles, CA

The author and publisher assume neither liability nor responsibility to any person or entity with respect to any direct or indirect loss or damage caused, or alleged to be caused, by the information contained herein, or for errors, omissions, inaccuracies, or any other inconsistencies within these pages, or for unintentional slights against people or organizations.

To my family, especially my wife, Helen, who helped me begin my business over 50 years ago and continues to be my greatest inspiration.

Contents

Acknowledgments xiii
Foreword xv
Introduction xvii

1. APPETIZERS
Bob Hope's Crunchy Broiled Grapefruit 1
Connie Stevens' Danish Cheese Buns 2
Wayne Newton's Spinach Salad With Hot Bacon Dressing 3
Lorne Greene's Deviled Ham Dip 4
Ronnie Schell's Power Cocktail 5
Diahann Carroll's Peachy Rhubarb 6
Anne Baxter's Peach-Ginger Cocktail 7
Tim Matheson's Fish-Cheese Tray 8
Howard Duff's Chive-Roquefort Spread 9
Bob Hope's Honeyed-Fig Grapefruit 10
Barbara Rush's Apple-Cheese Canapes 11
Dennis Cole's Dutch Herring Salad 12

Additional Appetizer Recipes
Apple Guacamole Delight 13
Roquefort-Stuffed Apples 13
Spicy Stuffed Prunes 14
Prune-Pretzel Party Mix 14
Mini Prune Sandwiches 15
Spinach Wok Salad 15
Bloody Mary Smoked Turkey Salad 16
Artichoke Relish Salad 17
Artichoke Squares 18
Honey-Cheese Dip 19
Blue Cheese-Wine Spread With Figs 19
Mini Smoked Salmon Monte Cristos 20
Smokey Salmon Spread 20
Sesame Pork Tidbits 21

2. SIDE DISHES
Phyllis Diller's Corn-Mushroom Saute 25
Frank Sinatra Jr.'s Sauteed Zucchini 26
Dennis Weaver's "There Ya Go" Vegetarian Dish 27
Bill Cosby's Prune-Nut Stuffing 28
Mickey Rooney's Kahlua Savory Stuffing 29
Juliet Mills' Raisin Stuffing 30

SIDE DISHES *(continued)*
Richard Long's Fresh Plum Sauce on Boiled Potatoes 31
Irene Ryan's Bavarian Apple Slaw 32
Elinor Donahue's Apple Stuffing 33
Juliet Mills' Minted Pineapple Stuffing 34

Additional Side Dish Recipes
Prune-Pineapple Stuffing Balls 35
Pumpkin Stuffing Balls 35
Broiled Apple Rings 36
Stuffed Baked Onions 36
Fig Stuffing Muffins 37
Fig Loaves 37
Stuffed Artichokes 38
Corn-Artichoke Flan 39
Artichoke-Chicken Pilaf 40
Olive Rice Olé 40
Ripe Olive Potato Salad 41
Chive-Bacon Brussels Sprouts 42
Peach Molds 42

3. ENTREES
Tony Randall's Crunchy Turkey Wraps 45
Bob Hope's Chicken With Citrus-Mustard Sauce 46
Jonathan Winters' Tuna Taipei 47
Phyllis Diller's Dill-Stuffed Sole 48
Jeanne Carmen's Shallot-Topped Fish With Wine Sauce 49
Frank Gorshin's Apple-Tuna Mold 50
Sid Caesar's Caesar-Style Fish 51
Karen Valentine's Bacon-Bundled Halibut 52
Francine York's Fillet a la Peche 53
Edward Mulhare's Ham With Old English Cheese Spread 54
Juliet Mills' Chive-Sausage Hoppin' John 55
Fred MacMurray's Barbecued Chuck Roast 56
Linda Crystal & Leif Ericson, Hangtown Fry 57

Additional Entree Recipes
Turf 'n Surf Teriyaki 58
Barbecued Shrimp Kebabs 58
Creole Snapper 59
Fish Polynesian 59
Chilean Chicken 60
Chicken Thighs With Saucepan Stuffing 61

ENTREES (continued)
Caribbean Lemon Chicken 61
Pineapple Chicken 62
Country Chicken With Peaches 62
Chicken "Cacciateriyaki" 63
Thai Cornish Hens 64
Honey-Glazed Turkey Strips 64
Turkey-Artichoke Stew 65
Turkey Provencale 66
Teri-Braten 67
Tomato-Beef Bake 67
Teriyaki Barbecued Chuck Roast 68
Mongolian Beef Pot 69
Ginger Lamb Stir-Fry 70
Lamb Patties With Gazpacho Sauce 71
Pork-Green Bean Stir-Fry 72
Fruit-Stuffed Pork Chops 73
Japanese Pork Chops 73
Pork Chop Casserole 74
Carrot-Sausage Casserole 74
Stuffed Ham Steaks 75

4. DESSERTS
Dinah Shore's Prune Whip & Port Wine 79
Jack La Lanne's Apple-Honey Pie 80
Bob Hope's Grapefruit Cobbler 81
Jeanette Nolan's Peach Crisp 82
Jill St. John's Strawberry-Crowned Pears 83
Rose Marie's Ice Cream Gelatin Mousse 84
Tim Matheson's Fruit-Marshmallow Sundae 85

Additional Dessert Recipes
Nut-Stuffed Prunes 86
Prune Crumble Pudding 86
Frozen Prune Delight 87
Chocolate Prune Bites 87
Peach Shortcake 88
Peach Alaska 88
Granny Apple Bars 89
Granny Apple Loaf Cake 90
Applesauce Nut Bread Ring 91
Strawberry "Flowerpots" 91

☆ ☆

DESSERTS *(continued)*
Fig Streusel Coffeecake 92
Gingered Figs 92
Fig-Carrot Roll 93
Fig Cookies 94
Fluffy Blueberry Pudding 95
Blueberry-Caramel Treat 95
Blueberry-Marshmallow Pie 96
Blueberry-Coconut Ice Cream Balls 96

Recipes of the Stars

By
Leo Pearlstein

Acknowledgments

While compiling all of the material for my autobiography, *Celebrity Stew: Food Publicity Pioneer Shares Over 50 Years of Entertaining Inside Stories of Hollywood Royalty*, I had so many behind-the-scenes stories and fantastic recipes, it would have been quite a huge book if I included everything. The wiser decision was to only include several recipes in the first book (from such stars as Bob Hope, Mickey Rooney, Phyllis Diller, Dinah Shore and Bill Cosby) and then come out with a follow-up book with just recipes I had developed to help draw extra attention to my clients' food products, in association with various celebrities. *Recipes of the Stars* is that follow-up book.

All of these recipes were developed and tested by the many professional and dedicated home economists, chefs, dieticians and nutritionists who worked over the years for the Western Research Kitchens division of my Los Angeles advertising and public relations agency, Lee & Associates, Inc. I wish to thank all of them most sincerely.

Also, my thanks go out to all of the wonderful and gracious celebrities and their managers and agents who helped arrange various publicity activities, and especially to Vic Parker, from the nationally distributed *TV/Movie News*, who put our *Recipe of the Week* together with photos of many of the biggest TV and movie stars that we used straight out of their pages.

Many thanks to Howard Pearlstein, who put in countless hours editing and supervising this entire project; Lisa Messinger, syndicated cookbook review columnist with Copley National News Service, who evaluated and edited each recipe to ensure they will be easy to prepare, as well as delicious and enjoyable for you; and Bill Goldfine, who supervised the creative production and helped tremendously with putting the book into its finished form.

LEO PEARLSTEIN

Foreword

☆ ☆

As I read recipe after recipe in this book, I had the urge to smuggle almost all of them—prepublication—to my mother. After all, there were treasures like muffins molded from stuffing, flecked with crumbles of crisp bacon and baked with crowns of whole dried figs to serve as a change of pace, nestled alongside turkey or broiled chicken; a nothing-less-than succulent pork chop casserole in which the meat snuggles with sauteed apples; and a grapefruit cobbler that had caught none other than Bob Hope's eye because of the indescribable sensation of a bite of butter, brown sugar and cinnamon-infused grapefruit and apple atop a flaky crust. That's when it struck me how truly special these recipes are.

Maybe I won't share them with my mother or anyone. I'll take all the credit at the next family gathering for my obvious talent and inventiveness.

Not once before had I ever thought recipes precious enough to hoard. As a matter of fact, I am the consummate sharer. For the last 10 years, I've told the world, or at least the millions of readers at the 750 newspapers to which my Copley News Service *Cooks' Books* column is syndicated each week, exactly what dishes I enjoy from the country's best cookbooks. I contribute lots more treats on my related web site, *Lisa Messinger Online: Your Cookbook Companion* at www.lisamessinger.com.

But this was a different story. My part in it began a few years ago when I first met Leo Pearlstein, as he was about to mark 50 years as the king of culinary public relations. Even though he's in the publicity business, Leo doesn't go around calling himself the king of culinary public relations and I found him by accident. Through a web of other food cover stories I was writing, I happened upon Leo, the man who had been hovering just outside the frame of hundreds of publicity stills with the likes of Bing Crosby, Abbott & Costello, Steve Allen, Dinah Shore, Fred MacMurray, Phyllis Diller, Shirley MacLaine and Groucho Marx, as they helped draw extra attention to turkeys, apples, potatoes or one of the dozens of other foods about which Leo, who had many of the food advisory boards as his clients, was responsible for letting the world know.

☆ ☆

This was also the man who booked more food-related guests (think Miss Chicken, Miss Prune and Miss Artichoke) on both the *Steve Allen Show* and with Dinah Shore, than anyone else. His omelet segment on *Dinah!*, Ms. Shore's 1970s talk show, was the longest food segment ever on television at the time (17 minutes), as Lucille Ball, Jimmy Stewart, Steve Lawrence and Eydie Gorme watched in awe as the world's fastest omelet-maker got all of these stars to make omelets.

Still, I had to convince Leo, the consummate behind-the-scenes man, that this time, after 50 years of intriguing stories like this, *he* was the story. I also asked him if he had ever thought of writing a book including his story, those vintage celebrity photos and the recipes his company had developed over the years, which serve as a virtual culinary history of the country from the 1950s to the present. He said it had crossed his mind, as two of his sons who work with him had been encouraging the idea for years, but he hadn't done anything serious about it yet because he was still so busy working daily with clients.

Fortunately, my encouragement was like the last ingredient needed to make a recipe work. His saucy *Celebrity Stew: Food Publicity Pioneer Shares 50 Years of Entertaining Inside Stories of Hollywood Royalty* (Hollywood Circle Press, $32.95 hardcover, $22.95 softcover; www.HollywoodCirclePress.com) is delightful and its foreword is a fond reminiscence by Steve Allen, that he wrote prior to his death in 2000. It makes me truly proud to have worked on this companion cookbook with Leo.

If you don't believe Leo Pearlstein is a part of this country's culinary history, just take a long look at the chives you chop and sprinkle over your baked potato or omelet and know you might not be doing that if it weren't for Leo. He introduced and publicized a number of now-common foods.

Leo's recipes are just too good to keep for myself under wraps. Read the book and I'm sure you'll agree.

LISA MESSINGER

Lisa Messinger is the syndicated cookbook
review columnist for Copley National
News Service

Introduction

☆ ☆

As I sat down to write this introduction, I did not plan any multimedia publicity blitz for this book. But, indirectly, it happens anyway almost daily. On TV alone, you can see Mickey Rooney (recipe page 29), as well as Bob Hope (recipe pages 1, 10, 46, 81), in classic films. Of course, many of the stars I worked with over 50 years are also still featured in movies, TV, print, stage and radio—everywhere you look.

Clearly, interest in the celebrities featured in this book is alive and well—just as I knew it would always be. I first got that feeling when I was working with legendary big-screen comedian Eddie Bracken in the 1940s at the advertising agency he owned as an investment with some of his earnings from classics like Preston Sturges' *The Miracle of Morgan Creek* and *Hail the Conquering Hero*. As a fresh-faced marketing man (from the first-ever class of marketing graduates at the University of Southern California), sure I was having fun at Bracken's, creating the first commercial for a frozen food product (a Chinese food entree) and other highs like that. But I quickly saw where the real action was. It was with Eddie and his celebrity pals. When he eventually closed shop and wished me well with my food clients, I thought there would be no better combination than matching the stars from Eddie's other campaigns with my food accounts, as well as courting new celebrities to do the same.

So what if no one before had put Abbott & Costello together with a 10-foot frying pan to promote eggs, or thought of casting a prune as Jack Webb's scene partner in an episode of *Dragnet*. Perhaps potato was never the secret word on Groucho Marx's hit game show *You Bet Your Life*, but we knew why it should have been when we got one of the growers of long whites (we represented the California Potato Advisory Board) on the show, telling Groucho about his livelihood. Groucho even posed for now-classic publicity stills with his secretary feeding him from one of the hundreds of jars of homemade potato salad he was given by fans after he mentioned he liked it while chatting with our client on the show.

These are just a few of hundreds of star-studded encounters I dreamed up (many chronicled in exciting, often side-splitting detail in my book *Celebrity Stew: Food Publicity Pioneer Shares 50 Years of*

☆ ☆

Entertaining Inside Stories of Hollywood Royalty, Hollywood Circle Press, www.HollywoodCirclePress.com). They certainly made for delicious stories, often delicious friendships and, most definitely, delicious recipes.

You see, while I was hard at work (that often seemed like play) corralling the stars and setting up our clients' product appearances, the exceptionally talented home economists at our Western Research Kitchens division of my Lee & Associates Public Relations & Advertising firm in Los Angeles were producing one spectacular recipe after another for the stars to help draw extra attention to our food clients' products. Just as the celebrities have stood the test of time and still stare back at us today from magazine covers and our TV screens, the recipes, too, emerge as dynamic as ever.

That's why, as I searched through my vaults of vintage recipes, I knew it was almost my duty to share them with you. They represent 50 years of our country's culinary history. However, they are nutritious, quick and easy—yet show-stopping—dishes. I'm including many of my favorite celebrity appetizer, side dish, main entree and dessert recipes, as well as additional favorites we created for many of my clients over the years.

I have a feeling that once you try them, were I to check back in with you after another 50 years in the culinary public relations business, these probably still would be among your family's all-time beloved recipes. There was good reason these were the stars' favorite recipes and I know you will enjoy them as much as they did. Therefore, in tribute to Groucho and all the other stars who contributed to my agency's success over the years, I'll make my anything-but-secret words be "Happy eating!"

LEO PEARLSTEIN

Appetizers

1
Appetizers

☆ ☆

Bob Hope, comedian, actor, humanitarian and general all-around great guy, created his annual golf tournament, *The Bob Hope Desert Classic,* in Palm Springs, California, for the benefit of various charities. We attended for years to help promote California grapefruit. It was always "showtime" for Hollywood stars, professional golfers and other celebrities who participated in this, the world's biggest golf tournament.

Bob Hope's Crunchy Broiled Grapefruit

2 grapefruits
½ cup crushed corn flakes
4 teaspoons melted butter
4 teaspoons brown sugar
½ teaspoon cinnamon

Halve grapefruit and loosen sections from membrane. Combine ingredients; sprinkle the mixture evenly over top of each half. Broil fruit until topping is golden brown. Serve immediately.

Yields 4 servings.

Connie Stevens is one of those rare personalities who was able to successfully transcend the entertainment gamut from motion picture star, television star, Broadway star, and recording artist to the concert stage. She has even gone beyond that to develop a successful cosmetic empire. Her original claim to fame was her endearing role as "Cricket Blake" in the hit TV series *Hawaiian Eye*. Also talented in the kitchen, following is a favorite appetizer recipe.

Connie Stevens'
Danish Cheese Buns With Fruit and Cheese Platter

2 egg whites
3½ ounces grated Gruyere or Cheddar cheese
Dash paprika
Vegetable oil, for frying
Dash celery salt
Assorted sliced cheeses, for serving
Assorted sliced fruits, for serving

Beat the egg whites until stiff. Add the grated cheese and paprika. Form into buns. Using a spoon, carefully place them in a pot of hot oil and fry them until they become golden brown. Lay them out on double paper towels; sprinkle with celery salt. Serve hot on a tray surrounded by the slices of cheese and fruit.

Yields 4 to 6 servings.

"Mr. Las Vegas" (aka Wayne Newton) sang his heart out beginning as a teen phenomenon and later sang the praises of spinach for us (this salad with hot bacon dressing is a sure thing). He rules the Strip (he's Sin City's highest-paid performer) and has made millions of fans happy over the decades with his millions-selling hits.

Wayne Newton's
Spinach Salad With Hot Bacon Dressing

1 large bunch fresh spinach
½ cup clear bacon drippings
3 teaspoons brown sugar
⅔ cup broken pieces crisp bacon
1 tablespoon fresh lemon juice
2 teaspoons red wine vinegar
Freshly ground black pepper, to taste, optional

Wash spinach well, deveining large leaves; draining well. Place in a salad serving bowl. Set aside. In skillet, carefully bring bacon drippings to sizzling point. Add brown sugar, stir to dissolve and add remaining ingredients, except pepper, stirring well. Pour sizzling hot dressing over spinach and mix. Serve with freshly ground black pepper, if desired.

Yields 2 large or 4 medium servings.

Many thought Lorne Greene had his hands full with his *Bonanza* Ponderosa ranch and his band of rugged sons on that hit show, but we knew better and utilized him to showcase chives, the herb with the mild onion flavor that we were first to introduce to the country.

**Lorne Greene's
Deviled Ham Dip**

1½ cups cottage cheese
1 (4.25-ounce) can deviled ham
2 tablespoons chopped chives

In a small mixing bowl, beat together cheese and ham until fairly smooth. Stir in chives. Cover and chill. Serve with chips and vegetables.

Yields 6 to 8 servings.

Believe it or not, Ronnie Schell—Gomer's scrawny cohort on *Gomer Pyle, USMC*—was the source for this nutritious power cocktail. He too, of course, was a powerhouse, first debuting as a standup comic in a showcase on Broadway before becoming a king of TV guest spots and commerical voiceovers.

Ronnie Schell's Power Cocktail

6 ounces cranberry juice
2 tablespoons oat bran
2 tablespoons wheat bran
1 tablespoon brewer's yeast
½ cup blueberries*
1 cup strawberries*
1 cup sliced or cubed mango* or papaya*
1 banana
1 tablespoon peanut butter
2 tablespoons protein powder
½ teaspoon vitamin C crystals
Pitted prunes, for serving

* Fresh or Frozen

Blend all ingredients until the consistency of a thick milk shake.

Yields 4 (6-ounce) servings.

APPETIZERS 5

☆ ☆

Although the peach-rhubarb appetizer she inspired definitely makes a splash, nothing was as significant as the splash made by Diahann Carroll when she starred in TV's *Julia*. The series, about a single mother working as a nurse while she raised her bright son, was the first time an African-American woman helmed a TV cast.

Diahann Carroll's Peachy Rhubarb

1 (15.25-ounce) can peach slices
½ pound rhubarb
½ cup sugar
Dash salt
4 to 6 sprigs fresh mint, or 1 teaspoon dried

Drain peaches, saving ¼ cup syrup. Cut rhubarb into ½-inch pieces. Pour peach syrup over rhubarb; add sugar and salt and simmer 5 minutes, until barely tender. Pour over peaches and chill thoroughly. Just before serving, top with mint. (Also good as an accompaniment for pork or duck; or over ice cream as a dessert.)

Yields 4 to 6 servings.

When we caught up with her to be in our peach campaign (just try and resist this appetizer cocktail), Anne Baxter was about to do a guest spot on TV's *Marcus Welby, M.D.* She already, though, was much acclaimed after playing a scheming protege in *All About Eve* and winning an Academy Award for *The Razor's Edge*.

Anne Baxter's Peach-Ginger Cocktail

1 (15.25-ounce) can peach slices
1 grapefruit
Dash salt
1 tablespoon finely chopped fresh ginger, or 1 teaspoon dried

Drain peaches, saving ¼ cup syrup. Pare and section grapefruit; squeeze juice from grapefruit shell. Blend peach syrup with salt and grapefruit juice. Arrange peaches in cocktail glasses. Pour grapefruit juice mixture over peaches. Chill. Top each serving with a grapefruit section and sprinkle with ginger.

Yields 6 servings.

☆ ☆

Tim Matheson says that, by far, his most recognizable role is that of Otter in the smash hit film *Animal House*. But when his photo accompanied our recipes in the *TV/Movie News* schedule guide, he was appearing on the popular small-screen series *The Virginian*. More recently, he played the vice president on NBC's Emmy-winning *The West Wing*.

Tim Matheson's Fish-Cheese Tray

Assorted Danish (such as samsoe, maribo, havarti) or other assorted cheeses, to taste
Smoked salmon, thinly sliced, to taste
Slivered onion, to taste
Celery hearts, to taste
Artichoke hearts, to taste
Caviar, to taste
Crackers, for serving

Slice cheese and wrap the smoked salmon around the slices, also including a sliver of onion in each packet. Place on a tray and surround with celery hearts, artichoke hearts, caviar and crackers.

8 APPETIZERS

When Howard Duff helped us take chives to a new level, he was starring on TV's *Felony Squad*. Prior to that was a distinguished career that began as he played Sam Spade of *Maltese Falcon* fame on radio and expanded to include Broadway and film roles, as well as a 20-year marriage to actress-director Ida Lupino.

Howard Duff's Chive-Roquefort Spread

¼ cup crumbled Roquefort or blue cheese
2 yolks from hard-cooked eggs
4 slices white bread, toasted
2 tablespoons chopped parsley
1 tablespoon chives

In a medium mixing bowl, combine cheese and egg yolks. Mix well. Spread on pieces of toast. Sprinkle with parsley and chives. Cut into finger strips, squares or triangles.

Yields about 8 (2-piece) servings.

Mr. Hope not only knew his way around the golf course, but his world travels were almost mythic. Here, he appears to be looking for the *Road to Entertaining the Troops*.

Bob Hope's Honeyed-Fig Grapefruit

6 dried figs
¼ cup honey
¼ cup water
3 grapefruits, cut into halves

Combine dried figs, honey and water in saucepan for sauce. Cover and simmer for 10 minutes. Cool. Cut around membranes of grapefruit to loosen, using a sharp paring knife. Cut each fig into 5 or 6 slices. Arrange one sliced fig on each half grapefruit. Spoon syrup over top. Garnish plate with extra figs, if desired.

Yields 6 servings

Barbara Rush has enjoyed a distinguished film career, embodying as varied choices as *Come Blow Your Horn* and the 3-D *It Came From Outer Space*. Her glowing beauty was a perfect complement to our apple promotion, including this snazzy canape recipe.

Barbara Rush's
Apple-Cheese Canapes

4 to 6 apples, mixture of red and green
16 slices white bread
1 (8-ounce) package cream cheese (preferably chive flavored)
Lemon juice, as needed
1 (8-ounce) tub sharp Cheddar cheese spread
20 black olives, pitted and quartered
16 sprigs parsley

Core apples; do not peel. Cut crosswise into 16 thin slices. Cut rounds from bread slices the same size as apple slices. Spread bread rounds with cream cheese. Place an apple slice on each round. Brush with lemon juice. Blend together Cheddar cheese spread and olives. Fill centers of apple with heaping teaspoonful of mixture. Top each with a parsley sprig.

Yields 16 canapes.

There are quite a few female viewers who wouldn't have minded being locked up with *Felony Squad* TV star Dennis Cole. He started his career as a dancer and stuntman and eventually appeared on Broadway and in many TV guest spots.

Dennis Cole's
Dutch Herring Salad

½ pound herring, diced
2 cups diced unpeeled red apples
1½ cups chopped onions
1½ cups sliced cooked potatoes
1½ cups diced cooked or canned beets
2 tablespoons capers, drained
½ cup mayonnaise
½ cup sour cream
Crisp salad greens, for serving

Combine all ingredients, except salad greens, in a large bowl and toss together thoroughly. Chill. Serve on the salad greens.

Yields 8 servings.

Apple-Guacamole Delight

1 ripe avocado
2 tablespoons lemon juice, plus more as needed
½ cup mayonnaise
1 small onion, minced
½ teaspoon salt
⅛ teaspoon Tabasco sauce
4 large red apples

Remove peel and pit from avocado; mash, beat or blend until smooth. Stir in lemon juice, mayonnaise, onion, salt and Tabasco sauce. Chill until ready to serve. Core apples; do not peel. Cut crosswise in 12 thick slices; dip in additional lemon juice. Cut each slice in bite-sized wedges; top with a mountain of avocado mixture.

Yields 12 servings

Roquefort-Stuffed Apples

1 (8-ounce) package cream cheese
¼ pound Roquefort or blue cheese
2 tablespoons dry white wine
8 small red apples
Assorted crackers, for serving

Combine cream cheese and crumbled Roquefort or blue cheese; beat until smooth, adding wine gradually. Cut thin slice from stem end of apples; reserve. Core apples, being careful not to cut all the way through. Scoop out pulp part way down. Fill with cheese mixture. Replace top slices. Chill thoroughly. Serve with assorted crackers.

Yields 8 servings.

Spicy Stuffed Prunes

½ (8-ounce) package cream cheese
2 tablespoons (preferably light) cream
2 cups ground baked ham
3 tablespoons mayonnaise
2 tablespoons pickle relish
1½ teaspoons finely chopped onion
½ teaspoon Worcestershire sauce
¼ teaspoon horseradish
¼ teaspoon prepared mustard
24 pitted prunes, cooked or microwaved to soften and then cut into halves
½ cup finely crushed corn chips

Mix cream cheese and cream. Set aside. Mix the ham with the mayonnaise, the next five ingredients and the cream cheese-cream mixture. Place a teaspoonful of ham mixture on each half of each prune. Top with crushed corn chips.

Yields 24 (2-piece) servings.

Prune-Pretzel Party Mix

1 stick butter
1 cup pitted prunes, chopped
½ teaspoon chili powder
½ teaspoon celery seed
½ teaspoon onion powder
3½ cups pretzel sticks
1 cup salted peanuts

Melt butter in large baking pan. Add chopped prunes and toss to coat. Add seasonings and stir. Add pretzel sticks and nuts. Mix. Bake in 275°F oven for 20 minutes, stirring once.

Yields 6 to 8 servings.

Mini Prune Sandwiches

Peanut butter
Chopped pitted prunes
Sour cream
White bread

Mix equal amounts peanut butter and chopped pitted prunes moistened with a little sour cream. Spread between slices of bread. Cut crust from each sandwich and then cut into sixths.

Spinach Wok Salad

1 bunch spinach, washed
3 tablespoons vegetable oil
1 tablespoon vinegar
2 teaspoons Dijon mustard
2 cloves garlic, minced
Salt, to taste
Pepper, to taste
1 bunch green onions, cut in 2-inch pieces
2 carrots, thinly sliced
1 tomato, cut in wedges
1 cup pitted black olives, whole or halved
1 avocado, sliced
½ cup walnut pieces

Remove spinach stems; tear into bite-sized pieces. Combine oil, vinegar, mustard, garlic, salt and pepper in wok or skillet over medium-high heat. Heat at 325°F for 2 minutes. Add onions and carrots; stir-fry 1 minute. Add remaining ingredients; stir-fry for 30 seconds. Cover and then carefully remove wok from heat. Leave covered 1 minute and then serve.

Yields 4 servings.

Bloody Mary Smoked Turkey Salad

1 tablespoon olive oil
1 tablespoon, plus 2 teaspoons, vegetable oil
2 tablespoons, plus 2 teaspoons, red wine vinegar
2 garlic cloves, minced
¾ teaspoon oregano
1 teaspoon salt
2 cups cooked smoked turkey breast, cut into strips or slices
½ cup bloody Mary seasoned tomato juice (or regular tomato juice, mixed with ¼ teaspoon black pepper)
8 drops Tabasco sauce
½ teaspoon lemon juice
¼ teaspoon Worcestershire sauce
1 head romaine lettuce, torn into bite-sized pieces
1 red onion, thinly sliced
1 green bell pepper, seeded, cut in half and sliced
3 tomatoes, cut in wedges

In a self-closing plastic bag, combine first 11 ingredients. Refrigerate 4 hours or overnight. Remove turkey from marinade. Reserve marinade for dressing. Arrange lettuce, vegetables and turkey on individual plates or serving platter. Top with dressing and serve.

Yields 4 servings.

Artichoke Relish Salad

1 (14-ounce) can artichoke hearts
⅓ cup red wine vinegar
1 clove garlic, minced
4 teaspoons chopped chives
½ teaspoon dry mustard
½ teaspoon basil
¼ teaspoon paprika
2 cups cherry tomatoes, cut in half
¾ cup (preferably pimento-stuffed) green olives, drained
½ cup pitted ripe black olives
1 cup sliced fresh mushrooms

Drain artichoke hearts; reserve liquid. In jar with cover, make dressing by combining the reserved liquid, vinegar, garlic, chives, mustard, basil and paprika; cover and shake well to blend. In large bowl, combine artichoke hearts, dressing, tomatoes, olives and mushrooms; toss gently.

Yields 6 servings.

Artichoke Squares

1 (14-ounce) can artichoke hearts
4 eggs
¼ cup dry breadcrumbs
¼ teaspoon oregano
¼ teaspoon hot pepper sauce
Salt, to taste
Pepper, to taste
1 cup minced onions
2 cups Cheddar cheese, grated (or 1 cup each Cheddar and muenster cheese, grated)
2 garlic cloves, minced
3 tablespoons minced parsley

Preheat oven to 325°F. Grease a 7 x 11-inch baking pan. In a medium skillet over medium heat, warm artichokes and their liquid until soft, about 5 minutes. Remove with slotted spoon; set aside. In large bowl, beat eggs. Stir in breadcrumbs, oregano, hot pepper sauce, salt and pepper. Chop artichoke hearts and add to egg mixture. Stir in onions, cheese, garlic and parsley. Mix well. Pour batter into prepared pan. Bake until golden, about 45 minutes. Cut into 1-inch squares and serve. Can be refrigerated and then reheated at 325°F for about 10 minutes.

Yields about 8 servings.

Honey-Cheese Dip

1 (8-ounce) package cream cheese
¼ cup cream or milk
2 tablespoons honey
1½ teaspoons vanilla extract
⅛ teaspoon nutmeg or mace
⅛ teaspoon cinnamon
2 tablespoons fresh lemon juice
¼ cup diced toasted almonds
Assorted fruits, for dipping

Blend together all ingredients, except almonds and fruit. Chill. When ready to serve, place in small bowl. Top with almonds. Place bowl on plate and surround with assorted fruits such as banana slices, melon cubes, grapes, strawberries and peach or nectarine slices for dipping.

Yields about 1 cup.

Blue Cheese-Wine Spread With Figs

6 ounces blue cheese, crumbled
1 (8-ounce) package cream cheese
¼ cup dry white wine
½ teaspoon Worcestershire sauce
½ teaspoon paprika
¼ teaspoon garlic powder
Few drops hot pepper sauce
Dried figs, for serving

In food processor or mixing bowl, blend cheeses. Blend in wine, Worcestershire sauce, paprika, garlic powder and hot pepper sauce. Serve at room temperature. If not serving immediately, refrigerate and then bring to room temperature. To serve: cut figs in half. Top each half with the blue cheese spread.

Yields about 1¼ cups.

Mini Smoked Salmon Monte Cristos

2 eggs, beaten
1 cup milk
1 teaspoon salt
1 teaspoon prepared mustard
Dash pepper
8 slices sourdough bread
1 (8-ounce) package cream cheese, softened
5 ounces smoked salmon
3 tablespoons chopped chives

Combine beaten eggs, milk, salt, mustard and pepper. Dip bread in egg mixture. Brown in sizzling skillet or griddle as for French toast. Turn four slices and brown on other sides. With a spatula, carefully turn other four slices and carefully spread with cream cheese, then sprinkle with chives. With a spatula, carefully remove all slices from heat. Top the four cream cheese topped slices with equal portions of smoked salmon and chives. Close each sandwich with non-spread bread. Cut each sandwich into eighths.

Yields about 10 (3-piece) servings

Smokey Salmon Spread

6 ounces sliced smoked salmon
1 (8-ounce) package cream cheese, softened
2 tablespoons cream
2 tablespoons lemon juice
Garlic powder, to taste
Crackers, for serving

Dice or chop the sliced smoked salmon. Combine with cream cheese, cream, lemon juice and garlic powder. Mix thoroughly and chill. Serve with crackers.

Yields about 8 servings.

Sesame Pork Tidbits

1½ pounds boneless lean pork loin
½ cup cornstarch
¼ cup teriyaki sauce
3 tablespoons sesame seeds, toasted
¼ cup sugar
¼ cup vinegar
¼ cup ketchup
¼ cup water
1 tablespoon teriyaki sauce
1½ teaspoons cornstarch
3 cups vegetable oil

Cut pork into 1-inch cubes. Thoroughly combine next 3 ingredients in bowl (mixture will be very stiff). Stir in pork; let stand 30 minutes. Meanwhile, combine next 6 ingredients in saucepan to make a sweet-and-sour sauce. Cook, stirring constantly, until thickened; set aside and keep warm. Carefully heat oil in saucepan over medium-high heat to 300°F. Carefully add ⅓ of the pork pieces and cook, stirring occasionally, until golden brown (approximately 2 minutes). Remove and drain thoroughly. Repeat with remaining pork. Serve immediately with warm sweet-and-sour sauce.

Yields approximately 18 (2-piece) servings

Side Dishes

2
Side Dishes

☆ ☆

Phyllis Diller is the first lady of American comedy—literally. A suburban housewife (for proof of her expertise in that area, just taste this delicious vegetable dish she inspired) helping to support her children, Ms. Diller used her natural comedic ability and quickly became the leading female stand-up comic. A TV variety show and films followed, not to mention her own very successful cookbook.

Phyllis Diller's Corn-Mushroom Saute

¼ cup butter or margarine
4 cups sweet corn kernels, fresh (about 8 ears), canned (drained) or frozen (thawed)
½ cup sliced green onions
⅛ cup chicken stock or water
2 cups sliced fresh mushrooms (about ½ pound)
Salt, to taste
Freshly ground black pepper, to taste
½ teaspoon dill weed

Melt butter or margarine in large skillet. Add corn, onion and chicken stock. Cook 3 minutes, stirring occasionally. Stir in sliced mushrooms and cook an additional 2 minutes. Just before removing from heat, season to taste with salt, pepper and dill weed. Serve immediately (if desired, cool and serve as a salad, adding 1 cup diced ham if this is to be a one-dish supper or the main dish for a luncheon).

Yields 6 servings.

Not just a junior to one of the 20th century's most famous men, Frank Sinatra, Jr. is a talented musician in his own right and also appeared often with his father. To boot, he is a good cook and a good sport in lending his presence to our zucchini promotion. He did us proud, when appearing alongside this outstanding fresh dish.

Frank Sinatra, Jr.'s Sauteed Zucchini

1 clove garlic, chopped
2 tablespoons olive oil
8 small zucchinis, unpeeled, cut into julienne sticks
½ teaspoon dried parsley
½ teaspoon dried basil
Salt, to taste
Pepper, to taste
4 tablespoons grated Parmesan or Romano cheese

Saute garlic in olive oil until brown, remove and discard. Add zucchini and saute. Add parsley and basil. Stir zucchini until the herbs have distributed throughout. Add salt and pepper. Top with about a tablespoon of cheese per serving.

Yields 4 servings.

☆ ☆

This simple—yet delicious—Western-inspired vegetarian dish seems to fit actor Dennis Weaver's down-home, friendly image like a glove. He was starring in TV's *McCloud* when we caught up with him. But, of course, before that he had created the unforgettable "Chester" character on *Gunsmoke* and appeared in a number of films. This is still one of his favorite recipes today, and here it is in his own words.

Dennis Weaver's "There Ya Go" Vegetarian Dish

1 large onion, chopped
2 stalks celery, chopped
1 tablespoon olive oil
6 organic tomatoes, chopped
¼ teaspoon fresh basil
¼ teaspoon fresh rosemary
1 tablespoon cumin
Salt, to taste
10 black olives, pitted and sliced
4 servings cooked rice or quinoa
2 cups canned beans (any kind), optional
1 shredded yam, optional
1 cup fresh corn kernels, optional

He says: "I start out by sauteing the chopped onion and celery in a little olive oil in a nonstick skillet. Then I add my homegrown tomatoes, with the fresh basil and rosemary. I stir in the cumin, salt to taste and simmer slowly about 10 minutes, or until the veggies are tender. If I want to add protein, I throw in the canned beans. Then I add sliced black olives and serve over cooked rice or quinoa. I've been known to add a shredded raw yam (for a little sweetness) or some fresh corn. Be creative!"

Yields 2 to 4 servings.

A TV pioneer, legend and still one of the most popular entertainers in show business, Bill Cosby starred in a number of TV shows (*I Spy*, *The Bill Cosby Show* and *Cos*) before steering *The Cosby Show* into TV and ratings history. And just like in every other area of his life, when he's cooking, it gets his full talent and attention.

Bill Cosby's Prune-Nut Stuffing

2 (6-ounce) bags packaged stuffing mix
1 cup butter
2 cups chopped prunes
1½ cups prune juice
10 to 14 pitted whole prunes
10 to 14 pecan halves

Combine dressing with butter, chopped prunes and pecans. Add liquid gradually. Mix ingredients. Stuff each whole prune with a pecan half. Place dressing in lightly greased 2-quart casserole, packing down lightly. Top with stuffed prunes and cover casserole with aluminum foil; press to seal. Bake at 325°F for 45 minutes, or until fully cooked.

Yields 8 to 10 servings.

This stuffing is decidedly interesting, but not quite as interesting as Mickey Rooney, its inspiration. The charismatic actor brought happiness to millions of moviegoers as Judy Garland's teen song-and-dance partner in a string of hits and then went on to bite off serious dramatic roles in films such as *Boys Town*, *Requiem for a Heavyweight* and *Bill*.

Mickey Rooney's Kahlua Savory Stuffing

8 ounces pork or turkey sausage
½ cup pecans, toasted and chopped
1 cup celery, diced
1 cup onions, diced
1 cup raisins
2 (6-ounce) bags Mrs. Cubbison's Stuffing
2 tablespoons parsley, minced
2 teaspoons grated orange zest
⅓ cup Kahlua
2 cups canned chicken broth

Cook sausage, breaking up the meat until browned. Remove from skillet and drain off drippings. Toast pecans by placing in a dry skillet on medium heat. Stir pecans in skillet for 5 minutes. cool and chop pecans. Mix remaining ingredients in a large bowl. Let stand to assure stuffing is moistened. Cool thoroughly before stuffing the turkey. Roast extra stuffing with the turkey the last 30 minutes of cooking in foil, rolled into the shape of a tube (twist ends closed), or bake 45 minutes at 350°F. Slice into small, round portions.

Yields 8 half-cup servings (three quarts stuffing; enough for a 12- to 14-lb. turkey).

As the magical nanny on TV's *Nanny and the Professor*, Juliet Mills' abilities included a lot more than cooking. But it was the versatile cooking skills of the actress (from England's famous Mills acting family, she had noteworthy roles on stage and screen, as well) we focused upon as we paired her with Mrs. Cubbison's Stuffing.

Juliet Mills' Raisin Stuffing

1 (6-ounce) bag Mrs. Cubbison's stuffing mix
½ cup melted butter or margarine
1 cup peeled, cored and chopped pippin apples
½ cup chopped onions
½ cup raisins
¾ cup apple juice

Combine stuffing mix with butter or margarine, apples, onions and raisins. Add apple juice gradually, blending lightly but thoroughly. Spoon into 2½- or 3-quart greased casserole; cover. Bake 30 to 45 minutes at 350°F, checking frequently near end. For crisper top, remove cover last 15 minutes.

Yields 4 servings.

☆ ☆

Richard Long had a long resume before appearing in his memorable role as the professor who was often in awe of his kids' nanny's magical powers in the hit TV show *Nanny and the Professor*. Among Long's other notable films, Orson Welles starred with and directed him in one of his early roles in *The Stranger*.

Richard Long's
Fresh Plum Sauce on Boiled Potatoes

1 pound fresh plums
¾ cup sugar
2 tablespoons cornstarch
¼ teaspoon cloves
¼ teaspoon cinnamon
¼ teaspoon allspice
1½ cups water
3 pounds small boiled potatoes

Cut plums in half; remove pits and slice. Combine sugar, cornstarch and spices. Gradually stir in water. Cook over medium heat until mixture begins to thicken. Add sliced plums, cover and simmer 10 minutes. Place hot potatoes in serving bowl. Drizzle sauce over potatoes.

Yields 2 cups sauce.

Best known, of course, as the irrepressible Granny on the popular *Beverly Hillbillies* TV series, versatile Irene Ryan also performed in films and on Broadway in such hits as *Pippin*. Granny was behind some truly wild concoctions, but this zesty standout slaw is more suited to the real Ms. Ryan.

Irene Ryan's Bavarian Apple Slaw

1 onion (preferably Spanish)
2 apples (preferably pippin)
4 cups shredded red cabbage
½ cup dill pickle slices
French dressing, to taste

Slice onion, separate into rings. Core apples, but do not peel; cut into thin slices. Combine onion, apple, cabbage and pickle. Chill. Just before serving, toss with French dressing.

Yields 6 servings.

First, Elinor Donahue was the oldest daughter in TV's *Father Knows Best* and then, the woman next door, as Andy Griffith's love interest on *The Andy Griffith Show*. Those sweet roles weren't far from the truth and that made Ms. Donahue a perfect match with our promotion for apples and for our oldest client, Mrs. Cubbison's Stuffing.

Elinor Donahue's Apple Stuffing

2 (6-ounce) bags packaged cornbread stuffing mix
1 cup melted butter or margarine
½ cup chopped celery
2 cups peeled, cored and chopped Granny Smith apples
½ cup chopped walnuts or almonds
1½ cups apple juice

Combine stuffing mix with butter or margarine, celery, apples and nuts. Stir apple juice in lightly. Spoon into 2½- or 3-quart greased casserole; cover. Bake 45 minutes at 325°F. For crisper top, remove cover last 15 minutes.

Yields 12 servings.

Juliet Mills'
Minted Pineapple Stuffing

1 (6-ounce) bag Mrs. Cubbison's cornbread stuffing mix
¼ cup chopped fresh mint
¼ cup brown sugar
1 cup crushed pineapple, drained
½ cup melted butter or margarine
¾ cup pineapple juice

    Combine stuffing mix with mint, brown sugar and pineapple. Blend in melted butter or margarine. Add pineapple juice and toss thoroughly but lightly. Spoon into greased 1½-quart casserole; cover. Bake at 325°F for 40 to 45 minutes. Garnish with a pineapple twist and a sprig of mint.

    Yields 4 servings.

Prune-Pineapple Stuffing Balls

1 (6-ounce) bag packaged cornbread stuffing mix
1 cup chopped, pitted prunes
1½ cups pineapple chunks, drained
½ cup sliced water chestnuts
⅛ to ¼ teaspoon curry powder, optional
½ cup melted butter or margarine
1 cup pineapple juice
8 to 10 pineapple slices

Combine stuffing mix with prunes, pineapple chunks, water chestnuts and curry powder. Blend in melted butter. Stir in pineapple juice, gently but thoroughly. Scoop into balls and place in a greased baking dish. Cover tightly with aluminum foil. Bake at 325°F for 30 to 40 minutes, or until firm. Serve atop the pineapple slices.

Yields 8 to 10 stuffing balls.

Pumpkin Stuffing Balls

1 (6-ounce) bag packaged stuffing mix
½ cup melted butter or margarine
1 cup mashed fresh or canned pumpkin
1 teaspoon allspice
¾ cups water
6 to 8 walnut halves

Combine stuffing mix with melted butter or margarine. Blend pumpkin with allspice; add to stuffing, reserving about 2 tablespoons for garnish. Blend in water, mixing well, but lightly. Shape stuffing into 6 or 8 balls and place in greased casserole. Top each with a teaspoon of reserved pumpkin and place a walnut half in center of each. Cover tightly with aluminum foil. Bake at 325°F for 35 to 45 minutes, or until firm.

Yields 6 to 8 stuffing balls.

Broiled Apple Rings

Red apples
Melted butter
Lemon juice
Cinnamon
Sugar

Peel and core as many apples as you would like to use. Cut into ¼-inch round slices. Set aside. For each 1 tablespoon of melted butter you use, mix in 1 teaspoon lemon juice. Brush this mixture on apple slices. Broil 5 minutes, turn, brush again with mixture and broil until golden brown. In a small bowl, mix together cinnamon and sugar, to taste. Sprinkle this mixture atop apple rings. Good served with chicken, turkey, lamb or pork.

Stuffed Baked Onions

8 large Spanish onions
1 (6-ounce) bag packaged cornbread stuffing mix
½ pound pork sausage, cooked
½ cup beef bouillon or water

Parboil onions for about 20 minutes and scoop out a large hollow in center of each. Combine stuffing mix with sausage and stir in liquid. Spoon stuffing into onions, mounding slightly on top. Place in lightly greased baking dish. Bake at 325°F for 1 hour, placing aluminum foil over onions if they brown too quickly.

Yields 8 servings.

Fig Stuffing Muffins

1 (6-ounce) bag packaged cornbread stuffing mix
½ cup melted butter or margarine
3 eggs, well beaten
1½ cups chicken broth
½ cup crumbled crisp cooked bacon
½ cup chopped dried figs
12 whole dried figs

Combine stuffing mix with melted butter or margarine, eggs, broth, bacon and chopped figs. Spoon mixture into 12 greased muffin cups. Top each muffin with a whole fig. Bake at 350°F for 30 to 35 minutes, or until firm. Cover muffins with aluminum foil if figs brown too quickly.

Yields 12 stuffing muffins.

Fig Loaves

2 (6-ounce) bags packaged cornbread stuffing mix
1 cup melted butter or margarine
1 cup chopped celery, including leaves
1 orange, chopped, including peel (seeds removed)
1 cup chopped dried figs
2 eggs, well beaten
1 cup milk

Combine all ingredients and mix until well blended. Pack mixture into 8 (4½ x 2½ x 1½-inch) greased loaf pans. Bake at 350°F for 35 minutes, or until firm to the touch. Unmold and serve.

Yields 8 single-serving loaves.

Stuffed Artichokes

4 large artichokes
1 tablespoon lemon juice
1 tablespoon butter
2 tablespoons all-purpose flour
½ cup dry white wine
½ cup heavy cream
Dash Tabasco sauce
Dash Worcestershire sauce
¼ teaspoon dry mustard
Salt, to taste
Pepper, to taste
½ cup crabmeat
1½ tablespoons butter
½ cup breadcrumbs

Cut stems from artichokes. Cook artichokes in 3 inches of boiling water with lemon juice for 25 to 35 minutes, or until a fork pierces the base easily. Cool; clip off thorny edges of leaves. Spread leaves carefully, remove center thistle portion with small spoon; discard. Melt the 1 tablespoon butter, add flour; let simmer for 5 minutes. Add wine and cream, stirring constantly; add Tabasco sauce, Worcestershire sauce, mustard, salt and pepper. Bring to a boil, lower heat and simmer for 10 minutes. Add crabmeat. Cook mixture for 7 minutes, then fill artichokes. Melt the 1½ tablespoons butter and combine with breadcrumbs. Top artichokes with breadcrumb mixture. Place in greased baking dish. Bake at 350°F until breadcrumbs brown.

Yields 4 servings.

Corn-Artichoke Flan

½ (14-ounce) can artichoke hearts
½ cup minced onions
1 cup whole kernel corn
2 tablespoons canned diced green chilies
4 eggs
2 cups cream, scalded (see note)
½ cup shredded Gouda or Cheddar cheese
¼ teaspoon chopped cilantro

Drain artichokes, reserving liquid; cut artichokes into large pieces. In medium saucepan, heat 2 tablespoons of the reserved liquid, add onion and saute until tender, about 5 minutes. Stir in corn and saute until liquid has evaporated. Add chilies and artichokes. Turn into greased 7 x 11-inch baking dish. In mixing bowl, beat eggs lightly. Beat in hot cream gradually (note: scalding is heating a liquid, often milk or cream, just below the boiling point), then return to the saucepan, whisking until blended. Stir in cheese. Pour over contents of baking dish. Sprinkle with cilantro. Set pan in a 9 x 13-inch pan and add one inch of boiling water. Bake at 300°F for 50 minutes, or until knife inserted in center comes out clean. Serve hot cut into squares.

Yields 12 servings.

Artichoke-Chicken Pilaf

2 chicken breasts, boned and cut into strips
1 clove garlic, minced
2 tablespoons butter or margarine
1¾ cups water
1 (6- to 7-ounce) package pilaf mix
½ teaspoon basil
1 (6-ounce) jar artichokes, drained, rinsed and halved
3 green onions, cut into ½-inch lengths
¼ cup toasted sliced almonds

Cook chicken and garlic in butter until browned. Carefully cut chicken into 1-inch pieces. Add water, contents of pilaf mix and basil. Bring to a boil. Reduce heat, cover and simmer 15 minutes. Stir in artichokes and green onions; cook 5 minutes more. Garnish with almonds.

Yields 4 to 6 servings.

Olive Rice Olé

1 cup sour cream
1 (4-ounce) can chopped green chilies
¼ teaspoon salt
3 cups cooked rice
1 cup shredded Monterey Jack cheese
1 cup pitted ripe olives, halved lengthwise
1 cup shredded Cheddar cheese

Combine sour cream, chilies and salt. In a 1½-quart casserole, layer in this order: half the rice, sour cream mixture, Monterey Jack cheese, half the olives, remaining rice and Cheddar cheese. Place remaining olives on top of the cheese. Bake at 350°F for 30 to 40 minutes, until hot and bubbly.

Yields 6 servings.

Ripe Olive Potato Salad

3 pounds new potatoes
1½ tablespoons vinegar
2 tablespoons vegetable oil
1½ teaspoons salt
¾ teaspoon dill weed
¼ teaspoon pepper
1⅔ cups pitted ripe olives
1 cup sliced celery
⅓ cup sliced green onion
1 (8-ounce) container plain yogurt
2 teaspoons prepared mustard
1 teaspoon honey
¼ teaspoon garlic salt

Cook potatoes in boiling salted water to cover until just tender. Cool sufficiently to handle. Peel and dice potatoes. Stir together vinegar, oil, salt, dill weed and pepper. Pour over potatoes and mix gently to coat. Chill. Meanwhile, drain olives well. Mix together ripe olives, celery and onion; add to potatoes. Mix together yogurt, mustard, honey and garlic salt; pour over potato salad and mix together gently but thoroughly.

Yields 6 to 8 servings.

Chive-Bacon Brussels Sprouts

1½ pounds frozen Brussels sprouts
6 strips bacon
¼ cup chopped chives
1 teaspoon salt
¼ cup sour cream
Paprika, for garnish

Wash sprouts. Follow package cooking instructions and cook just until tender, or cover sprouts with 1 cup water and cook, covered, 8 to 10 minutes, just until tender. While sprouts are cooking, fry bacon until crisp; drain on paper towels and crumble when cool. Combine crumbled bacon, chives and salt with sour cream. Drain sprouts and pour over sour cream mixture. Reduce heat to low and cook, but do not boil, until sour cream is heated through. Sprinkle with paprika.

Yields 6 servings.

Peach Molds

1 egg
2 tablespoons sugar
3 tablespoons lemon juice
6 marshmallows, diced
½ cup sour cream
1 package lemon-flavored gelatin
1 cup hot water
1½ cups sliced fresh peaches

Beat egg slightly; add sugar. Gradually add lemon juice, stirring while adding. Cook over very low heat until mixture thickens, stirring constantly. Add marshmallows and stir until melted. Cool and fold in sour cream. Dissolve gelatin with hot water. Cool until slightly thickened; fold in egg mixture. When cold, fold in peaches. Turn into 1 large or individual molds and allow to set (usually takes at least a few hours to set).

Yields 6 servings.

Entrees

3
Entrees

☆☆☆☆☆☆☆☆☆☆☆☆☆☆☆☆☆☆☆☆☆☆☆☆☆☆☆

Tony Randall was the fussbudget half of TV's hit *The Odd Couple*, but there's nothing odd about this crunchy (apples, celery and tortilla chips) recipe he inspired. Before that, he was inspiration for Rock Hudson and other top stars in a string of memorable film roles and was lauded for his multiple roles in *7 Faces of Dr. Lao*.

Tony Randall's Crunchy Turkey Wraps

1 cup diced cooked turkey
½ cup diced celery
½ cup diced pippin (or other) apple
½ cup mayonnaise
¼ cup diced sweet pickles
1 tablespoon lemon juice
1 cup lightly crushed tortilla chips
4 flour tortillas
½ cup Cheddar cheese

Mix ingredients, except tortillas and cheese, in order given. Place equal portions of mixture atop tortillas. Sprinkle with cheese and wrap up tortillas. Heat at 200°F for 10 minutes, or until slightly heated through.

Yields 4 servings.

Bob Hope did it all with aplomb—legendary stand-up comedy, blockbuster films and brilliantly entertaining our toops abroad for decades. He epitomized the phrase "legend in his own time." Hats off to a gentleman who gave show business a good name.

Bob Hope's
Chicken With Citrus-Mustard Sauce

½ cup freshly squeezed grapefruit juice
1 cup grape jelly
2 tablespoons lemon juice
½ teaspoon grated grapefruit zest
½ teaspoon grated lemon zest
1½ teaspoons dry mustard
⅛ teaspoon confectioner's (powdered) sugar
1 tablespoon cornstarch
Seasoned salt, to taste
1 cup grapefruit sections
4 chicken breasts, cooked and kept warm

Combine all ingredients, except grapefruit sections and chicken. Bring to a boil, stirring, and simmer a few minutes until thickened. Add grapefruit sections and heat thoroughly. Serve atop chicken.

Yields 4 servings.

Jonathan Winters is a one-man theatrical troupe. His improvisational genius instantly creates characters, voices, sound effects and stories to entertain his audiences. He has been on countless TV shows and in movies and has created an array of cartoon voices. He is also an author and painter. This recipe is a complement to his creativity, as well.

Jonathan Winters' Tuna Taipei

1 (12-ounce) can tuna
½ cup chopped green onion
¼ cup vegetable oil
4 cups cold unsalted cooked rice
3 tablespoons soy sauce
2 eggs, beaten
1 (8-ounce) can water chestnuts, drained and chopped

Drain and flake tuna. Cook onion in hot oil in a skillet until tender. Add rice and soy sauce. Stir over low heat until rice is hot. Push rice to one side. Pour in eggs and cook thoroughly, stirring frequently. Add water chestnuts and tuna. Mix well and heat.

Yields 6 servings.

Phyllis Diller didn't just joke in her successful stand-up act about her looks, her husband and her children, but about her cooking ability, as well. She's actually an excellent gourmet cook in her own right.

Phyllis Diller's Dill-Stuffed Sole

3 pounds fillet of sole or halibut
1 (6-ounce) bag Mrs. Cubbison's cornbread stuffing mix
¼ cup melted butter
¼ cup chopped dill pickles
¼ cup minced onion
Salt, to taste
Pepper, to taste
1 egg, beaten
2 tablespoons or less dry white wine
1 onion, sliced very thin
1 tomato, sliced very thin
Sweet basil, to taste

Butter a shallow baking dish and place half the fish in it. Make stuffing by combining and mixing the cornbread stuffing, melted butter, dill pickle, minced onion, salt, pepper, beaten egg and enough wine to moisten to your desired consistency. Spread the stuffing over the fish in the baking dish. Top with remaining fish. On top of fish, arrange thin onion slices, then tomato slices. Sprinkle with salt and pepper and sweet basil. Bake about 40 minutes at 350°F, or until fish is thoroughly cooked and flakes with a fork.

Yields 6 to 8 servings.

After arriving in Hollywood in the early 1950s, Jeanne Carmen started appearing in movies and was quite an item at all the celebrity parties. She was often in the company of the town's most notable swingers, such as Elvis and Sinatra. She also maintained a close relationship with Marilyn Monroe. While she never made it into major movies, she became known as Queen of the "B" movies.

Jeanne Carmen's Shallot-Topped Fish With Wine Sauce

2 pounds fish fillets
1½ teaspoons salt
½ teaspoon pepper
2 tablespoons chopped shallots
2 tablespoons chopped parsley
1 cup dry white wine
2 tablespoons fresh breadcrumbs
½ stick butter

Arrange fish fillets in shallow baking dish that also can be a serving dish. Dust fillets with salt and pepper; sprinkle with shallots and parsley. Pour wine around fish, being careful not to wash off the seasoning. Sprinkle breadcrumbs over fish and dot with butter. Bake at 450°F about 15 minutes until fish is thoroughly cooked and top is brown.

Yields 4 to 6 servings.

☆ ☆

Talented performer Frank Gorshin has appeared in movies, on television and on Broadway. It was his role as "The Riddler" on the TV series "Batman," for which he received an Emmy nomination, that changed his professional career. His talents also shine in the kitchen. Following is one of his favorite quick and easy entree recipes.

Frank Gorshin's Apple-Tuna Mold

1 (3 ounce) package lemon-flavored gelatin
1 cup boiling water
¼ teaspoon salt
Dash of pepper
1 cup cold water
2 tablespoons lemon juice
1 (6½ or 7½ ounce) can tuna, flaked
½ cup chopped celery
½ teaspoon paprika
1 cup diced unpeeled apples

Dissolve gelatin in boiling water. Add salt, pepper, cold water and lemon juice. Chill until slightly thickened. Fold in tuna, celery, paprika and apples. Turn into 5-cup mold. Chill until firm. Unmold and serve with mayonnaise or salad dressing.

Yields 6 servings.

Sid Caesar was famous for *Your Show of Shows* pioneering live TV comedy series. So, take this as your "fish of fish" recipe, cleverly customized with Caesar salad dressing. No, Sid Caesar didn't create that famous dressing, but he helped create just about everything having to do with classic TV comedy.

Sid Caesar's Caesar-Style Fish

2 pounds fish fillets
½ cup Caesar salad dressing
1 cup crushed potato chips
½ cup shredded sharp Cheddar cheese

Dip fillets in salad dressing. Place fillets in a single layer, skin side down, in a baking dish. Combine crushed chips and cheese. Sprinkle over fillets. Bake at 500°F for 10 to 15 minutes, or until fillets are thoroughly cooked and flake easily with a fork.

Yields 6 servings.

This is a bundled recipe and Karen Valentine, who appeared in our seafood promotion, is famous for playing a bundle of joy. Perky and friendly (on TV and in real life), the appropriately named Valentine fronted a number of TV series, including, of course, *Room 222*, and is currently appearing in productions on and off-Broadway and in regional theaters.

Karen Valentine's Bacon-Bundled Halibut

1½ pounds halibut
¼ cup lemon juice
¼ cup vegetable oil
Salt, to taste
Pepper, to taste
Garlic powder, to taste
Oregano, to taste
8 strips bacon

Combine all ingredients, except bacon. Marinate fish in mixture overnight in refrigerator. When ready to serve, wrap strips of bacon around fish; secure with toothpicks. Broil until bacon and fish are thoroughly cooked, about 8 minutes.

Yields 6 servings.

If ever there is a peach, it's lovely Francine York and, therefore, it's appropriate she heped us educate home cooks about fish with this outstanding peach-topped fillet recipe. It was Jerry Lewis who first dubbed Ms. York peachy, by discovering her and starring her in six films, including *The Nutty Professor*. Lots more film and TV roles followed.

Francine York's Fillet a la Peche

1 pound cod or sole fillets
½ cup condensed skim milk
¼ cup canned sliced mushrooms
1½ teaspoons seasoned salt
Dash pepper
⅛ teaspoon thyme
⅛ teaspoon tarragon leaves
Dash paprika
1 bay leaf
¼ cup breadcrumbs
2 teaspoons melted butter
6 to 8 cling peach slices
2 teaspoons chopped chives

Place fish fillets in shallow baking pan. Cover with milk, mushrooms and seasonings. Bake at 375°F for 8 minutes, or until almost done. Meanwhile, mix together breadcrumbs and melted butter. Sprinkle over fillets. Arrange peach slices on top. Sprinkle with chopped chives and a dash of paprika. Bake 2 to 3 minutes longer, or until fish is thoroughly cooked and flakes with a fork.

Yields 4 servings.

The acting of this Hollywood pro was much more complex than the easy, yet delicious, recipe Edward Mulhare inspired for ham steaks topped with fruit-infused cheese. Of course, he was the anything-but-invisible ghost on TV's *The Ghost and Mrs. Muir*, but also graced the screen and stage, including replacing Rex Harrison in *My Fair Lady*.

Edward Mulhare's
Ham With Old English Cheese Spread

1 (8-ounce) container sharp Cheddar cheese spread
10 prunes, cooked and finely chopped
Dash fresh lemon juice
Dash garlic powder
6 ham steaks, cooked and kept warm

Mix cheese with prunes until spread is soft; add lemon juice and garlic powder. Spread atop ham steaks.

Yields 6 servings.

☆ ☆

Juliet Mills had a lot of special effects to think about while playing the part of a nanny with special powers on ABC's hit *Nanny and the Professor*. But that doesn't mean her thoughts didn't sometimes drift to her next culinary creation. We loved featuring the products we represented alongside this exceptionally nice nanny.

Juliet Mills'
Chive-Sausage Hoppin' John

1½ pounds sausages
1 green bell pepper, chopped
1 (15-ounce) can kidney beans, drained
3 cups cooked rice
¼ cup, plus 1 tablespoon, chopped chives
1 (6-ounce) can tomato paste
1 (1-pound) can tomatoes, chopped
Salt, to taste
Pepper, to taste

Fry sausages until lightly browned. Saute green bell pepper in ¼ cup of sausage drippings. Combine green pepper mixture with remaining ingredients, except the 1 tablespoon chives. Pour mixture into 1½-quart casserole. Top with sausages. Bake at 400°F for 25 to 30 minutes, or until hot and bubbly. Sprinkle the top with the additional chives.

Yields 6 servings.

Uncle Charlie sure could have used this super-simple barbecue recipe for the never-ending appetites of Fred MacMurray's ravenous three sons on the long-running hit TV series *My Three Sons*. Nice guy MacMurray was a perfect fit to help us sell the public on the flavor and convenience of this entree.

Fred MacMurray's Barbecued Chuck Roast With Chives

1 chuck steak, 2 inches thick, about 4 pounds
Salt, to taste
Garlic powder, to taste
2 cups red wine (preferably MacMurray Ranch brand Pinot Noir)
2 tablespoons chopped chives
1 bay leaf
6 peppercorns
¼ cup olive oil
2 tablespoons soy sauce
Toasted buns, for serving

Rub steak with salt and garlic powder. Place steak into a shallow pan. Pour over red wine, chives, bay leaf, peppercorns, olive oil and soy sauce. Let stand at room temperature 2 hours, turning occasionally. Drain and broil 6 inches above gray coals for about 20 minutes on each side (until meat is thoroughly cooked), brushing with marinade from pan every 10 minutes. Cut into very thin slices and serve on toasted, crusty buns.

Yields 8 servings.

Linda Crystal and Leif Ericson, popular TV and film actors, were among the guests who enjoyed these "Hangtown Fry" omelets. We recreated the omelets for the very successful "Gold Miners Breakfast" that our clients hosted in Placerville, California, to promote several food products.

Chive Hangtown Fry

12 oysters
¼ cup butter or margarine
6 eggs
¼ cup light cream
¼ cup chives
Salt, to taste
Pepper, to taste

Shuck oysters and saute in butter until edges curl. Beat eggs and cream together. Pour mixture over oysters. Sprinkle with chives. Cook over low heat, stirring constantly until mixture is scrambled, but still moist. Season with salt and pepper. Good served with a crisp salad and slices of hot toast.

Yields 6 servings.

Surf 'n' Turf Teriyaki

½ pineapple
1 pound sirloin steak
10 large shrimp
¼ cup soy sauce
¼ cup honey
3 tablespoons brandy
1 clove garlic, minced
1 teaspoon grated orange zest
3 green onions
1 green bell pepper
1 tablespoon cornstarch
2 tomatoes, cut into 5 wedges each

Remove fruit from pineapple shell and cut into 10 chunks. Cut steak into 10 cubes, removing fat. Shell shrimp, leaving tails on. Combine soy sauce, honey, brandy, garlic and orange zest. Marinate steak and shrimp 3 to 4 hours in refrigerator. Drain; reserve marinade. Cut onions into 10 pieces. Cut green bell pepper into 10 squares. Skewer a pineapple chunk, shrimp, green onion, steak cube and green bell pepper square on each of 10 skewers. Blend cornstarch into reserved marinade; heat to boiling, stirring constantly, until thickened. Place skewers on barbecue grill. Brush with marinade. Grill over moderately hot coals 3 minutes. Turn, add a tomato wedge to each skewer; brush with marinade. Broil 3 to 5 minutes longer. Serve immediately.

Yields 10 servings.

Barbecued Shrimp Kebabs

4 slices bacon, quartered
1 pound shrimp in shells, fresh or frozen
12 whole tiny onions
1 green bell pepper, cut into 1½-inch squares
1 cup barbecue sauce
4 cherry tomatoes, optional

Fold each quarter piece of bacon in half. On skewers, alternate shrimp with bacon, onions and green bell pepper squares. Press ends of each piece of bacon against the shrimp and onion. Bacon creates a self-basting effect; but leave ends of skewers free of bacon because it may char. Arrange skewers on barbecue grill and brush liberally with barbecue sauce. Broil over moderately hot coals 5 minutes on each side, brushing frequently with sauce. Add cherry tomatoes to skewers the last few minutes of cooking.

Yields 4 servings.

Creole Snapper

- 2 pounds fresh or frozen red snapper fillets (unfrozen)
- 6 tablespoons teriyaki sauce
- 4 tablespoons lemon juice
- 1 tablespoon vegetable oil
- ½ cup diced celery
- ½ cup diced green bell pepper
- ½ cup diced onion
- 1 tablespoon Tabasco sauce
- 1 cup diced tomatoes

Cut fillets into serving portions; drain thoroughly if thawed. Mix 4 tablespoons teriyaki sauce and 1 tablespoon lemon juice in large shallow pan. Arrange fish, in single layer, in sauce. Marinate 15 minutes in refrigerator; turn over once. Bake fish in sauce at 350°F 12 to 15 minutes, until thoroughly cooked and until fish flakes with fork. Meanwhile, heat oil in large frying pan. Add next three ingredients; saute over medium heat until tender, yet crisp. Stir in remaining teriyaki sauce, lemon juice and Tabasco sauce; bring to a boil. Add tomatoes; cook only until heated through, stirring constantly. To serve: remove fish from sauce and top with tomato mixture.

Yields 6 servings.

Fish Polynesian

- 1 pound fish fillets
- All-purpose flour, for dusting fish
- ½ cup melted butter or margarine
- 3 tablespoons frozen orange juice concentrate, thawed
- 1 tablespoon chopped parsley
- 2 teaspoons chopped chives
- 1 teaspoon salt
- Pinch cayenne pepper
- ½ teaspoon paprika
- 3 tablespoons toasted slivered almonds

Dust fish with flour; place in a greased 1½-quart casserole. Combine melted butter or margarine with orange juice concentrate, parsley, chives, salt and cayenne; pour over fillets. Broil 8 to 10 minutes, basting occasionally with sauce, until thoroughly cooked and fish flakes with a fork. To serve: sprinkle top lightly with paprika and almonds.

Yields 4 servings.

Chilean Chicken

1½ cups green seedless grapes
8 large frying chicken pieces
2 tablespoons all-purpose flour
1 teaspoon salt
¼ teaspoon pepper
2 tablespoons vegetable oil
3 tablespoons butter
1 clove garlic, minced
½ cup chopped onion
¼ cup chopped red or green bell pepper
1 (14.5-ounce) can stewed tomatoes
½ teaspoon coriander
4 drops red pepper sauce
3 tablespoons vinegar
1½ cups canned chicken broth
1 tablespoon cornstarch
1 tablespoon cold water
2 tablespoons finely chopped mint or parsley

Rinse grapes and remove stems. Dredge chicken in flour mixed with salt and pepper. Brown slowly in oil and 1 tablespoon butter until golden on both sides. Meanwhile, cook garlic, onion and bell pepper in remaining 2 tablespoons butter over low heat until soft, but not browned. Add tomatoes, coriander and hot pepper sauce. Simmer 5 minutes. Add vinegar and chicken broth. Drain and discard any excess fat from browning chicken. Spoon sauce over chicken, cover and simmer 20 minutes. Remove cover and continue cooking until chicken is tender and thoroughly cooked, about 10 to 15 minutes. Add grapes. Blend cornstarch with water and stir into pan sauce. Simmer a few minutes until thickened. Taste and add salt, if needed. Add mint or parsley.

Yields 6 servings.

Chicken Thighs With Saucepan Stuffing

2 teaspoons poultry seasoning
1¼ cups water
2 tablespoons butter or margarine
1 (6-ounce) bag packaged stuffing mix
8 chicken thighs
1 tablespoon melted butter
Salt, to taste
Pepper, to taste

Combine poultry seasoning with water and butter or margarine in saucepan. Bring to a boil, reduce heat, cover pan; simmer 4 minutes. Uncover, stir in stuffing mix. Cover, let stand 5 minutes. Remove cover, fluff with fork. Cool slightly. Lift skin on each thigh and pat stuffing mix between meat and skin. Pull skin over stuffing. Arrange on baking sheet skin side up. Brush chicken skin with melted butter and season with salt and pepper. Bake at 350°F 35 to 45 minutes, or until thoroughly cooked and juices run clear when pierced with a fork.

Yields 8 servings.

Caribbean Lemon Chicken

1 (3-pound) broiler chicken, quartered
½ cup teriyaki sauce
1 teaspoon grated lemon zest
1 tablespoon lemon juice
2 teaspoons hot pepper sauce
¼ teaspoon cinnamon

Place chicken quarters in large plastic bag. Combine teriyaki sauce, lemon zest and juice, hot pepper sauce and cinnamon; pour into bag over chicken. Press air out of bag; close top securely. Turn over several times to coat chicken. Refrigerate 8 hours, turning bag over occasionally. Remove chicken from marinade and place on rack in broiler pan. Broil 5 to 7 inches from heat 20 to 25 minutes on each side, or until chicken is tender, thoroughly cooked and juices run clear when pierced with a fork.

Yields 4 servings.

Pineapple Chicken

4 chicken thighs
¾ cup teriyaki sauce
¼ cup unsweetened pineapple juice

Rinse and pat dry thighs, leaving skins intact. Place in a large plastic bag. Combine teriyaki sauce and pineapple juice. Pour mixture over chicken into bag; press air out, close top securely. Refrigerate 8 hours or overnight, turning bag over occasionally. Remove from marinade; place on grill 6 inches from moderate coals. Cook about 35 minutes, or until thoroughly cooked and juices run clear when pierced with a fork.

Yields 4 servings.

Country Chicken With Peaches

¼ cup all-purpose flour
¼ teaspoon garlic powder
3 pounds frying chicken pieces
2 tablespoons vegetable oil
1 (15.25-ounce) can sliced peaches
½ cup teriyaki sauce

Combine flour and garlic powder; coat chicken thoroughly with mixture. Brown chicken on all sides in hot oil in Dutch oven or large skillet over medium heat. Drain off fat. Drain peaches; reserve ½ cup syrup. Combine syrup with teriyaki sauce and ¼ cup water; pour over chicken. Bring to a boil; reduce heat and simmer, covered, 30 minutes. Turn over chicken pieces. Simmer, covered, 15 minutes longer, or until chicken is tender, thoroughly cooked and juices run clear when pierced with a fork. Arrange peaches around chicken; heat through. Remove chicken and peaches to serving platter. Skim off excess fat from pan juices and serve the remaining pan juices with chicken and peaches.

Yields 4 to 6 servings.

Chicken "Cacciateriyaki"

3 pounds frying chicken pieces
¼ cup olive oil or vegetable oil
1 large onion, sliced
2 cloves garlic, minced
1 (14.5-ounce) can tomatoes
1 (8-ounce) can tomato sauce
⅓ cup teriyaki sauce
1 teaspoon oregano
2 bay leaves
Cooked spaghetti or noodles, for serving

Brown chicken thoroughly in hot oil in large deep skillet or Dutch oven; remove. Add onion and garlic to oil; cook until onion is translucent. Stir in remaining ingredients; arrange chicken pieces in sauce. Cover and simmer 45 minutes, or until chicken is tender, thoroughly cooked and juices run clear when pierced with a fork. To serve: Place chicken on bed of spaghetti or noodles. Discard bay leaves and skim off excess fat from sauce; serve sauce atop chicken.

Yields 4 to 6 servings.

Thai Cornish Hens

3 Cornish hens (1¼ to 1½ pounds each)
1½ cups teriyaki sauce
1 tablespoon grated lemon zest
1 tablespoon lemon juice
2 cloves garlic, minced
¼ teaspoon cayenne pepper
1 tablespoon minced cilantro, optional

    Remove and discard giblets and necks from hens, if necessary. Split hens lengthwise. Rinse halves under cold running water; drain well and pat dry with paper towels. Combine teriyaki sauce, lemon zest and juice, garlic and cayenne pepper; pour over hens in large plastic bag. Press air out of bag; close top securely. Turn bag over several times to coat hens. Refrigerate 8 hours, turning bag over occasionally. Reserving marinade, remove hens and place on grill 5 to 7 inches from hot coals. Cook 45 to 50 minutes, until drumsticks remove easily and hens are thoroughly cooked. Turn hens over frequently and brush with reserved marinade. Remove to serving platter and sprinkle with cilantro.

    Yields 4 to 6 servings.

Honey-Glazed Turkey Strips

½ cup honey
¼ cup butter or margarine, melted
2 teaspoons grated lemon zest
2 tablespoons lemon juice
½ teaspoon dill weed
1 pound turkey breast strips, cooked

    Combine all ingredients, except turkey. Brush honey mixture over turkey strips. Reheat turkey to heat glaze.

    Yields 4 servings

Turkey-Artichoke Stew

1 cup tiny boiling onions
1 cup carrot chunks
1½ cups canned chicken broth
1 tablespoon all-purpose flour
¼ teaspoon paprika
¼ teaspoon salt
¾ pound turkey breast slices
1 (6-ounce) can artichoke hearts
1 teaspoon lemon juice
2 teaspoons cornstarch
½ teaspoon prepared mustard
1 tablespoon chopped parsley

Combine onions, carrots and chicken broth. Bring to a boil and simmer, covered, until barely tender. Meanwhile combine flour, paprika and salt. Roll turkey slices in seasoned flour to coat lightly. Spoon a tablespoon of artichoke liquid into large nonstick skillet and heat. Add turkey slices and stir-fry over moderately high heat, until tender, thoroughly cooked and juices run clear when pierced with a fork, about 3 minutes. Add broth, including the vegetables. Stir lemon juice, cornstarch and mustard into a tablespoon of the artichoke liquid. Add artichokes with remaining liquid to turkey. Stir in cornstarch mixture and cook a few minutes longer to heat and thicken slightly. Sprinkle with parsley.

Yields 4 servings.

Turkey Provencale

½ turkey breast (about 2 pounds), skinned and boned
3 tablespoons soy sauce
⅛ cup all-purpose flour
4 tablespoons vegetable oil
¼ cup thinly sliced green onions
1 garlic clove, minced
½ cup dry white wine
2 medium tomatoes, cut into wedges
2 tablespoons minced parsley

Slice turkey breast lengthwise into 4 equal pieces. Place each piece between sheets of waxed paper; pound gently and evenly until about ¼-inch thick. Coat both sides of pieces with 2 tablespoons of the soy sauce; let stand 30 minutes in the refrigerator. Lightly coat with flour. Heat 2 tablespoons of the oil in a large skillet over medium heat. Carefully cook 2 of the turkey pieces in hot oil 4 to 5 minutes on each side, or until golden brown and tender, thoroughly cooked and juices run clear when pierced with a fork. Remove to serving platter; keep warm. Repeat with remaining oil and turkey. Add green onions and garlic to skillet; saute over high heat 30 seconds. Add wine and boil 1 minute. Add tomatoes, parsley and remaining soy sauce. Carefully cook and stir over medium heat 2 minutes; serve over turkey pieces.

Yields 4 servings.

Teri-Braten

1 (3½-pound) beef chuck roast
2 tablespoons vegetable oil
½ cup teriyaki sauce
3 tablespoons cider vinegar
¼ cup all-purpose flour
⅛ teaspoon pepper

Brown both sides of roast thoroughly in hot oil in large deep skillet or Dutch oven. Combine teriyaki sauce, vinegar and 1⅓ cups water; pour over roast. Cover and simmer 1 hour. Turn roast over and simmer, covered, 1 hour longer or until thoroughly cooked. Remove from pan; set aside and keep warm. Pour drippings into large measuring cup. Skim off 3 tablespoons fat; return to pan. Stir in flour until blended. Add enough water to remaining drippings to measure 2¾ cups; stir into flour mixture with pepper. Cook until mixture boils and thickens, stirring constantly. To serve: carve meat across grain into thin slices and serve with gravy.

Yields 6 servings.

Tomato-Beef Bake

3 cups noodles
1 pound ground beef
1 onion, sliced
2 cloves garlic, minced
3 tomatoes, sliced
1 green bell pepper, sliced
¼ cup soy sauce

Cook noodles in boiling, salted water according to package directions; drain. Brown beef until thoroughly cooked with onion and garlic; cook until onion is translucent. Add tomatoes, green bell pepper and soy sauce; stir to combine. Bring to boil and cook only until tomatoes are heated through. Stir in noodles; turn into 2-quart baking dish. Bake, uncovered, at 350°F for 20 minutes.

Yields 6 servings.

Teriyaki Barbecued Chuck Roast

1 (3½-pound) beef chuck roast, 1 to 1½ inches thick
½ cup teriyaki sauce
1 onion, chopped
½ cup chopped green bell pepper
1 tablespoon vegetable oil
1 tomato, chopped
1 tablespoon soy sauce
¼ teaspoon Tabasco sauce

Place meat in large plastic bag; pour in teriyaki sauce. Press air out of bag; tie top securely. Turn over to coat both sides. Refrigerate 8 hours, turning bag over occasionally. Remove meat, reserve marinade. Place meat on grill 6 inches from hot coals and cook about 20 minutes on each side (for medium), check for doneness; or longer for desired degree of doneness. Make sure meat is thoroughly cooked. Meanwhile, combine reserved marinade with enough water to measure ⅔ cup; set aside. Saute onion and green bell pepper in hot oil, until onion is translucent. Stir in marinade mixture; simmer 1 minute. Stir in tomato, soy sauce and Tabasco sauce; bring to a boil. Carve meat across grain and serve with sauce.

Yields 6 servings.

Mongolian Beef Pot

4 tablespoons soy sauce
2 teaspoons minced fresh gingerroot
½ teaspoon sugar
1½ pounds sirloin steak, cut into 1-inch cubes
3 cups canned beef broth
1 clove garlic, minced
½ pound cabbage, cut into ¾-inch chunks
¾ pound fresh spinach, trimmed, washed and drained
3 green onions, cut into slivers
4 ounces vermicelli or spaghetti, cooked
¼ pound mushrooms, sliced, optional

Combine 2 tablespoons soy sauce, ginger and sugar in bowl. Stir in beef; let stand 10 minutes. Combine beef broth, 4 soup cans full of water, remaining 2 tablespoons soy sauce and garlic in wok or deep skillet; bring to a boil. Reduce heat; keep broth mixture hot. Arrange beef and next 5 ingredients on large platter. Using chopsticks, forks or tongs, let diners select and carefully add beef and vegetables to hot broth; cook until meat is thoroughly cooked. Serve meat and vegetables in individual bowls with additional soy sauce; discard broth.

Yields 4 to 6 servings.

Ginger Lamb Stir-Fry

1 pound ground lamb
3 tablespoons vegetable oil
1 cup sliced onion
1 clove garlic, minced
2 cups thinly sliced celery
2 cups broccoli florets
1 cup thinly sliced red or green bell pepper
2 tablespoons cornstarch
2 cups beef broth
1¼ teaspoons ground ginger
¾ teaspoon salt
½ cup diced tomato

In wok or large skillet, brown ground lamb until cooked through. Drain. Remove lamb and set aside. Carefully heat oil in the wok or skillet until hot. Add onion and garlic; stir-fry for 30 seconds. Add celery, broccoli and bell pepper. Stir-fry until broccoli is barely crisp-tender, about 4 minutes. Combine cornstarch and broth; stir in ginger and salt. Carefully pour into wok. Cook and stir until thickened, about 1 minute. Stir in lamb and tomatoes; heat until hot.

Yields 4 servings.

Lamb Patties With Gazpacho Sauce

1 (28-ounce) can peeled whole tomatoes or 1½ pounds fresh tomatoes, peeled
3 cucumbers, peeled and chopped
3 green onions, chopped
1 green bell pepper, chopped
2 cloves garlic, minced
2 stalks celery, chopped
½ teaspoon dill weed
1 tablespoon sugar
16 ounces tomato juice
¼ cup lemon juice
1 teaspoon salt
Tabasco sauce, to taste
¼ teaspoon paprika
1½ pounds ground lamb
Sour cream, for serving
Chopped parsley, for serving

    Combine all vegetables with olive oil, dill weed and sugar. Pour into large container and mix with tomato juice, lemon juice, salt, Tabasco sauce and paprika. Refrigerate 24 hours to blend flavors (do not freeze). Before serving: divide ground lamb into 6 portions and form patties. Broil or grill until completely cooked. Meanwhile, bring gazpacho to room temperature. Place cooked patties on 6 dinner plates. Top with gazpacho, then a dollop of sour cream and a sprinkling of parsley.
    Yields 6 servings.

Pork-Green Bean Stir-Fry

1 pound pork shoulder chops, boned
2 tablespoons cornstarch
4 tablespoons soy sauce
1 tablespoon dry sherry
1 clove garlic, minced
1 cup water
2 tablespoons vegetable oil
1 (12- to 16-ounce) package frozen (preferably French-style) green beans, thawed and drained
2 carrots, peeled and cut into thin diagonal slices
4 fresh mushrooms, sliced

Slice pork into thin strips. Combine 1 tablespoon each cornstarch and soy sauce with sherry and garlic; stir in pork. Let stand 30 minutes in the refrigerator. Meanwhile, blend together remaining cornstarch and soy sauce with water; set aside. Heat 1 tablespoon oil in wok or large skillet over high heat. Add pork and stir-fry about 4 minutes, or until golden brown and meat is thoroughly cooked; remove. Heat remaining oil in same pan; add green beans and carrots and stir-fry about 3 minutes, or until vegetables are tender-crisp. Stir in pork, mushrooms and soy sauce mixture; bring to boil. Cook 2 minutes, or until sauce thickens. Serve immediately.

Yields 4 servings.

Fruit-Stuffed Pork Chops

6 dried figs, finely chopped
1 large red apple, cored and diced
1/8 teaspoon nutmeg
6 double pork chops, cut with pockets
Salt, to taste
Pepper, to taste
1 cup chicken broth

Mix figs and apple with nutmeg; stuff into pockets of pork chops. Sprinkle with salt and pepper. Brown both sides of chops in large hot skillet. Reduce heat; add bouillon. Cover and simmer for 50 to 60 minutes, or until meat is completely cooked.

Yields 6 servings.

Japanese Pork Chops

6 boneless pork loin chops, 1/2 to 3/4-inch thick
1/2 cup teriyaki sauce
1/3 cup all-purpose flour
1 egg, beaten
1/2 cup dry breadcrumbs
3 tablespoons vegetable oil

Trim any excess fat from pork chops. Marinate in teriyaki sauce 20 minutes in refrigerator; turn over and marinate 20 minutes longer. Remove chops from marinade; coat both sides of each chop with flour, then dip into egg and then coat thoroughly with breadcrumbs. Heat oil in skillet over medium-low heat. Carefully add chops and cook for 20 minutes. Turn chops and cook 15 minutes longer, or until chops are golden brown and thoroughly cooked.

Yields 6 servings.

Pork Chop Casserole

3 red apples
6 boneless pork loin chops, ½- to ¾-inch thick
½ cup butter or margarine
¾ cup vegetable or beef broth or water (or use part apple juice, if desired)
1 (6-ounce) bag packaged cornbread stuffing mix

Core apples. Chop two of the apples; slice the third. In a large skillet, brown pork chops on both sides. In same skillet, melt butter; add broth and chopped apples. Simmer about 1 minute. Place stuffing mix in a greased, shallow baking dish. Pour apple mixture over stuffing; toss to blend completely. Arrange browned pork chops over stuffing and tuck in sliced apple between pork chops. Cover with aluminum foil; bake at 350°F for 35 to 40 minutes, or until pork chops are fork-tender and thoroughly cooked.

Yields 6 servings.

Carrot-Sausage Casserole

1 (6-ounce) bag packaged stuffing mix
¼ cup chopped onion
¼ cup butter
¼ cup chopped parsley
1 cup grated carrots
¾ teaspoon caraway seeds
½ pound ground pork sausage, browned
1 egg
½ cup sour cream

Empty stuffing mix into bowl. Saute onion in butter until transparent. Add to stuffing mix. Blend in parsley, grated carrots, caraway seeds and browned sausage. Beat egg, toss into stuffing mixture. Add sour cream and blend. Spoon in greased 1½-quart casserole. Cover and bake at 325°F 30 to 45 minutes. Garnish with some grated carrots and parsley, if desired.

Yields 4 to 6 servings.

Stuffed Ham Steaks

2 thick ham steaks
¼ cup cloves
2 (6-ounce) bags packaged cornbread stuffing mix
1 (16-ounce) can pineapple slices
¼ teaspoon dry mustard
2 tablespoons brown sugar

Score the edges of ham steaks with clean kitchen scissors; stud edges with cloves. Place 1 slice in 2-quart baking dish. Top with a layer of stuffing prepared according to package instructions with two additions: 1) Use all but ¼ cup pineapple juice in place of equal amount of water in stuffing (reserve the ¼ cup juice); 2) Chop half the pineapple slices into bite-sized pieces and mix into stuffing. Save unused stuffing for stuffing balls (see below). Top layered ham steak with the other ham steak. Prepare basting sauce by combining reserved ½ cup juice, dry mustard and brown sugar. Brush meat with sauce; cover baking dish with aluminum foil. Bake at 350°F for 1½ hours; baste occasionally. Remove cover during last 20 minutes to brown ham. Make sure ham is thoroughly cooked.

Roll remaining stuffing into small balls. Place in greased baking pan. Bake for the last 45 minutes of the cooking time. Use remaining pineapple slices to garnish serving platter.

Yields 6 servings.

Desserts

4
Desserts

☆ ☆

As her many friends tell it—and viewers got to see often on *Dinah!*, her 1970s talk show—Dinah Shore was the real thing: an unparalleled gourmet cook. This elegant whipped port wine-infused dessert is worthy of Ms. Shore, who first made it big as a singer before moving on to film roles and her own popular TV variety shows.

Dinah Shore's Prune Whip & Port Wine

½ pound pitted prunes
⅔ cup granulated sugar
3 lemon slices, with rind
1 cup port wine
1 cup whipping cream
1 tablespoon confectioner's (powdered) sugar
Almonds, blanched, slivered and toasted

Place prunes, sugar and lemon slices in a saucepan. Cover with water and bring to a boil. Simmer for 5 minutes. Drain (save the juice). Leave prunes in pan and add most of the wine and cook 10 minutes longer. Puree the prunes in a blender or with electric mixer. Add remaining port wine or the reserved prune juice to keep the prunes moist. Whip the cream and mix half with the prunes. Sweeten remaining cream with confectioner's sugar and use as a garnish. Sprinkle top with almonds.

Yields 4 servings.

Jack La Lanne has been a glowing example of fitness and vitality for a good part of the last century. That's why we were so proud to team with him to help promote the healthful aspects of apples. Of course, since we were working with Mr. La Lanne, that meant an especially healthful recipe with whole wheat pastry flour and honey, rather than refined sugar.

Jack La Lanne's Apple-Honey Pie

Pastry for a double-crust 9-inch pie
5 to 7 baking apples
¾ to 1 cup honey
2 tablespoons whole wheat pastry flour
⅛ teaspoon salt
1 teaspoon cinnamon
¼ teaspoon nutmeg
1 tablespoon lemon juice or grated lemon peel, if necessary

Line a 9-inch pie pan with bottom pastry. Pare apples and slice thin. Add honey and mix with whole wheat flour, salt and spices. Place filling in the pastry-lined pan. Brush pastry with vegetable oil. Adjust top crust. Bake at 450°F for 10 minutes, then at 350°F 40 minutes. If apples are not tart enough, add 1 tablespoon lemon juice or grated lemon peel.

Yields 10 to 12 servings.

When you make this citrus cobbler at home (inspired by our days with Bob Hope in grapefruit-rich Coachella Valley), it won't make you want to hit the road as Mr. Hope did with Bing Crosby in all those hilarious *Road to...* films. Our pairing of juicy grapefruit and sweet apples may not quite compare to their legendary screen pairing, but it comes close!

Bob Hope's Grapefruit Cobbler

Pastry for single-crust 8-inch pie
2 cups grapefruit sections
¾ cup brown sugar, packed
1 teaspoon cinnamon
3 tablespoons cornstarch
1 (21-ounce) can apple pie filling
2 tablespoons butter

Roll out pastry for 8-inch round greased pie pan; cut 2-inch circle in center. Drain grapefruit sections. Combine brown sugar, cinnamon and cornstarch; mix gently with apple pie filling and heat to boiling, stirring carefully as needed. Add butter, then grapefruit. Heat, but do not boil. Place fruit mixture in baking dish. Arrange pastry on fruit and flute edges. Bake at 425°F for about 20 minutes, or until nicely browned.

Yields 6 to 8 servings.

Jeanette Nolan was guest starring on TV's *The Virginian* when *TV/Movie News* published her lovely photo with our wonderful fresh peach-graham cracker crisp. Ms. Nolan was, of course, well known for her film (*The Man Who Shot Liberty Valance* with James Stewart and John Wayne) and TV roles (*The Real McCoys*).

Jeanette Nolan's Peach Crisp

- 4 fresh peaches, peeled, pitted and sliced
- 1 tablespoon lemon juice
- ½ cup sugar
- ½ cup graham cracker crumbs
- ½ cup slivered almonds
- 1 teaspoon cinnamon
- 2 tablespoons butter

Spread peaches in 9-inch pie pan. Drizzle with lemon juice. Mix sugar, graham cracker crumbs, almonds and cinnamon. Sprinkle over peaches. Dot with butter. Bake at 350°F 30 minutes. Serve warm or cold with cream or ice cream.

Yields 4 to 6 servings.

☆ ☆

As husband Robert Wagner and her fans know, Jill St. John is a gem. Appropriately, then, when we featured her with this creative dessert, she was filming the James Bond film *Diamonds Are Forever* with Sean Connery. Ms. St. John began as a child star in more than 1,000 radio shows and appeared at age 10 in the first TV movie ever filmed.

Jill St. John's Strawberry-Crowned Pears

1 cup fresh strawberries
2 tablespoons sugar
¼ cup cream
2 (15.25-ounce) cans sliced pears

Slice strawberries. Sprinkle with sugar. Beat cream until it is stiff. Fold in strawberries. Drain pears; chill. Before serving, top pears with strawberry-cream mixture.

Yields 6 servings.

Talk about "staying power," Rose Marie began her career in entertainment at the age of 3 as Baby Rose Marie. By the time she was 5, NBC signed her to star in her own national radio show. Her classic character, "Sally Rogers" on the *Dick Van Dyke Show*, earned her three Emmy nominations and if that didn't give her enough exposure, among all the movies and countless TV shows on which she appeared over the years, she also came into everyone's home in America as a celebrity contestant on many popular TV game shows. She appeared a record 14 years as a regular on *The Hollywood Squares*. She's quite talented in the kitchen, too.

Rose Marie's Ice Cream Gelatin Mousse

2 (3 ounce) packages gelatin
2 pints vanilla ice cream
1 pint strawberries
Whipped cream

Prepare gelatin according to package directions. (Use either raspberry, cherry or strawberry flavor.) Refrigerate until just set. Add 2 pints of vanilla ice cream and whip together until gelatin and ice cream are foamy and fluffy.

Remove stems from strawberries, leaving the stems on a few of the berries for the top. Fold the berries into the gelatin/ice cream mixture. Pour into dessert glasses and chill until set. Just before serving, top each dessert glass with whipped cream and a strawberry.

Yields 6 to 8 servings

Watch out—Tim Matheson, who played the vice president on the multiple Emmy-award-winning show *The West Wing*, just might give you an executive order to try this dynamic sundae he inspired. We helped publicize Mr. Matheson's career way back when he was appearing on TV's *The Virginian*.

Tim Matheson's Fruit-Marshmallow Sundae

1 (15-ounce) can fruit cocktail
1 cup miniature marshmallows
1 tablespoon fresh lemon juice
¼ teaspoon almond extract
Dash salt
Vanilla ice cream

Combine all ingredients, except ice cream. Chill at least 1 hour. Serve atop ice cream.

Yields 2 cups topping.

Nut-Stuffed Prunes

18 prunes
18 walnuts
30 marshmallows
¼ cup butter or margarine
½ teaspoon vanilla extract
5 cups crisp rice cereal

   Rinse prunes and place in colander over boiling water. Steam 10 to 15 minutes. Cool. Remove pits and stuff each with a piece of walnut. Cut marshmallows into quarters and place in saucepan with butter or margarine. Set over hot water and heat until marshmallows are completely melted. Stir in vanilla extract. Place cereal in large buttered bowl; pour marshmallow mixture over it, tossing lightly to coat cereal. Let cool a few minutes. With buttered hands, shape rice mixture around stuffed prunes.

   Yields 18 stuffed prunes.

Prune Crumble Pudding

1½ cups pitted prunes, cooked
Juice of 1 lemon
¼ cup liquid from prunes
6 tablespoons all-purpose flour
¼ cup firmly packed dark brown sugar
2 tablespoons shortening
1 teaspoon salt

   Place prunes in greased 1-quart shallow baking dish. Add lemon juice and prune liquid. Work remaining ingredients together to consistency of fine crumbs; sprinkle over prunes. Bake at 375°F for 20 minutes. Serve warm with milk.

   Yields 4 servings.

Frozen Prune Delight

1 cup undiluted evaporated milk
⅓ cup sugar
Dash salt
½ cup fresh orange juice
1 teaspoon fresh lemon juice
1 cup pitted prunes, cooked and chopped

    Put evaporated milk in freezer until nearly frozen. Beat until stiff. Add sugar, salt and continue beating until no grains of sugar remain. Fold in juices and fruit. Freeze.

    Yields 4 servings.

Chocolate Prune Bites

1 (1-pound) package pitted prunes
2 cups semisweet chocolate chips
2 cups marshmallow cream
½ teaspoon cinnamon
Coconut, to taste
Chopped nuts, to taste
Chocolate sprinkles, to taste

    Cut prunes open. In top of double boiler, melt chocolate over hot, but not boiling, water. Blend in marshmallow cream and cinnamon. When cool, shape into balls; roll in coconut, nuts or chocolate sprinkles. Stuff into prunes.

    Yields 8 to 10 servings.

Peach Shortcake

1 package spice cake mix
1 (15.25-ounce) can sliced peaches
1 cup cream
Red cinnamon candies, for garnish, optional
Mint sprigs, for garnish, optional

    Prepare spice cake mix according to package directions. Bake in 9-inch layers. Cool. Drain peaches thoroughly. Whip cream. Put whipped cream and peaches between cake layers and on top. Decorate with cinnamon candies and mint sprigs.
    Yields 10 to 12 servings.

Peach Alaska

6 fresh peaches, peeled, pitted and halved
Juice of 1 lemon
Vanilla ice cream
Confectioner's (powdered) sugar, for dusting
Brandy, optional

    Slightly even off bottom of 6 of the peach halves so that they can sit steadily on a serving plate. Coat peaches with lemon juice. Quickly fill those 6 bottom halves of peaches with small scoops of ice cream. Top with remaining peach halves to form whole peach shapes. Hold together with toothpick. Dust with powdered sugar and splash with brandy. Serve immediately.
    Yields 6 servings.

Granny Apple Bars

2 cups sugar
2 cups all-purpose flour
2 teaspoons cinnamon
1 teaspoon baking soda
½ teaspoon salt
3 cups peeled, cored, coarsely chopped Granny Smith apples
1 cup chopped walnuts or pecans
3 eggs
½ cup vegetable oil
2 teaspoons vanilla extract
1 (8-ounce) package cream cheese
3 tablespoons butter or margarine
2 teaspoons vanilla extract
1½ cups confectioner's (powdered) sugar
Pinch of salt

Sift together sugar, flour, cinnamon, baking soda and salt. Add to apples along with the chopped nuts. Beat the eggs, oil and 2 teaspoons vanilla extract until foamy and add to the apple mixture. Pour into a 9 x 13-inch greased pan and bake at 350°F for 45 to 60 minutes, or until a knife inserted in center comes out clean. Blend together cream cheese, butter or margarine, vanilla extract, powdered sugar and salt. Pour this mixture over warm cake. Cool; cut into bars.

Yields 10 to 12 servings.

Granny Apple Loaf Cake

1½ sticks butter or margarine
1⅔ cups sugar
2 eggs, beaten
2 cups all-purpose flour
¼ teaspoon cinnamon
¼ teaspoon salt
1 teaspoon baking soda
1 teaspoon baking powder
2 cups peeled, cored, finely chopped Granny Smith apples
1 cup walnuts or pecans
1 cup raisins or chopped dates
1 teaspoon vanilla extract

    Cream together butter or margarine, sugar and eggs until light and fluffy. Sift together the flour, cinnamon, salt, baking soda and baking powder. Add to creamed mixture and blend well. Stir in the apples, nuts and raisins or dates. Add vanilla extract. Pour into 2 greased and floured loaf pans and bake at 350°F for 35 to 45 minutes, or until a knife inserted in center comes out clean.

    Yields 14 to 16 servings.

Applesauce Nut Bread Ring

3 cups all-purpose flour
⅔ cup sugar
3½ teaspoons baking powder
½ teaspoon baking soda
1½ teaspoons salt
½ teaspoon cinnamon
1 cup chopped walnuts or pecans
1 egg, beaten
1 (14-ounce) jar applesauce
3 tablespoons shortening

Sift together dry ingredients; stir in nuts. Add egg, applesauce and shortening. Mix just until blended. Turn batter into a greased 1½-quart ring mold (or a 9 x 5-inch loaf pan), spreading batter evenly. Bake at 350°F for 50 to 55 minutes (60 to 65 minutes if using loaf pan), or until a knife inserted in spots comes out clean. Turn out and cool on a wire rack.

Yields 12 to 14 servings.

Strawberry "Flowerpots"

1 (12-ounce) can evaporated milk
1½ tablespoons grated lemon zest
½ cup lemon juice
2¼ cups strawberry preserves

Pour milk into ice cube tray; chill in freezer until crystals form around edges. Pour into bowl and whip until stiff. Carefully fold in lemon zest, juice and ½ cup of the preserves. Spoon into large mugs within one inch of tops. Insert a half length of clear drinking straw into center of each mug. Place in freezer to freeze firm. To serve: Slip artificial or fresh flowers into straws. Spread preserves over top of each frozen dessert. Serve immediately.

Yields 6 servings.

Fig Streusel Coffeecake

¼ cup butter
½ cup firmly packed brown sugar
⅓ cup all-purpose flour
2 teaspoons cinnamon
1 cup coarsely chopped dried figs
¼ cup margarine
¾ cup sugar
2 eggs
1½ cups all-purpose flour
2 teaspoons baking powder
½ cup milk

Mix together butter, brown sugar, cup flour and cinnamon to make a crumbly mixture. Mix in figs until well coated. Set aside. Beat margarine until smooth and creamy. Beat in sugar gradually; add eggs one at a time. Stir in flour and baking powder. Add to bowl alternately with milk. Turn into greased 9-inch round pan. Sprinkle fig mixture evenly on top of batter. Bake at 375°F for 25 minutes, or until knife inserted in center comes out clean. Best served hot or warm.

Yields 8 to 10 servings.

Gingered Figs

18 dried figs
3 cups water
1 tablespoon molasses
2 teaspoons powdered ginger
½ cup sugar
Vanilla ice cream

Place figs and water in saucepan. Bring to hard boil, then lower heat and simmer. Cover figs and cook for 20 minutes. Add molasses, ginger and sugar. Stir gently in order to avoid breaking figs. Simmer for 15 minutes more, or until figs are plumped and tender. Cool. Serve with ice cream.

Yields 6 servings.

Fig-Carrot Roll

1 cup finely chopped dried figs
½ cup diced almonds
½ (8-ounce) package cream cheese, softened
½ cup sweetened condensed milk
½ teaspoon grated lemon peel
½ teaspoon vanilla extract
¾ cup sugar
½ cup oil
2 eggs
1 cup all-purpose flour
1 teaspoon baking powder
1 teaspoon baking soda
1 teaspoon cinnamon
½ teaspoon nutmeg
½ teaspoon salt
2 cups grated carrots
Confectioner's (powdered) sugar, for garnish

Line a 10 x 15-inch jellyroll pan with aluminum foil and oil lightly. Combine figs and almonds; sprinkle in bottom of pan. Combine cream cheese with sweetened condensed milk, lemon peel and vanilla extract. Pour over figs and almonds; set aside. Cream sugar, oil and eggs. Combine flour, baking powder, baking soda, cinnamon, nutmeg and salt. Stir dry ingredients into creamed mixture; mix well. Stir in carrots; mix well. Pour batter into prepared pan. Bake at 350°F for 25 minutes. Sprinkle cake with confectioner's sugar. Cover with towel or waxed paper. Invert onto cookie sheet; gently remove foil. Roll cake tightly, starting from short side; don't worry if a few rolls tend to crack. Cool completely before removing towel from top.

Yields 8 to 10 servings.

Fig Cookies

1 cup dried figs
2 cups all-purpose flour
2 teaspoons baking powder
½ teaspoon salt
1 teaspoon cinnamon
2 cups quick-cooking oats
½ cup chopped walnuts or pecans
¾ cup shortening
1 cup brown sugar
2 eggs, well beaten
8 tablespoons water

   Cover figs with hot water; allow to stand 10 minutes. Pour off water and reserve. Snip off stems from figs, then chop coarsely. To the flour, add baking powder, salt and cinnamon. Add oats, figs and nuts. Cream shortening; add brown sugar and cream together thoroughly. Add eggs and then the dry mixture alternatively with 8 tablespoons of the reserved water to form dough. (Use more or less water as necessary.) Drop by teaspoonfuls on greased cookie sheet. Bake at 400°F for 10 minutes.

   Yields 4 dozen cookies.

Fluffy Blueberry Pudding

1 package vanilla pudding mix
2 egg whites
2 tablespoons sugar
1 cup frozen blueberries, thawed

Prepare vanilla pudding mix according to package directions. Remove from heat and cool slightly. Beat egg whites until stiff, gradually adding sugar. Continue until mixture holds stiff peaks. Fold into pudding with blueberries. Chill. Serve plain or over slices of angel food cake.

Yields 4 to 6 servings.

Blueberry-Caramel Treat

1 pound frozen blueberries, partially thawed
2 tablespoons cornstarch
½ cup sugar
10 caramel candies, melted
Vanilla ice cream

Drain all juice from partially thawed blueberries and add enough water to equal ¾ cup liquid. Add liquid to mixture of cornstarch and sugar. Simmer about 5 minutes, or until translucent and thick. Gradually add melted caramel. Fold in berries; chill. Serve spooned over vanilla ice cream.

Yields 6 to 8 servings.

Blueberry-Marshmallow Pie

½ pound marshmallows
½ cup milk
1 cup heavy cream, whipped
1 teaspoon vanilla extract
¼ teaspoon salt
2 cups frozen blueberries, thawed and drained
1 baked 9-inch pie shell

Melt marshmallows in milk over hot water. Cool, beating out lumps. Do not allow to congeal. Fold in whipped cream, vanilla and salt. In pie shell, arrange alternate layers of marshmallow mixture and blueberries, beginning and ending with marshmallow. Chill at least 1 hour before serving.

Yields 8 to 10 servings.

Blueberry-Coconut Ice Cream Balls

1 pound frozen blueberries, partially thawed
1 cup sugar
1 tablespoon lemon juice
1 teaspoon butter or margarine
1 pint vanilla ice cream
2 cups shredded or flaked coconut

Crush blueberries, reserving some whole ones for garnish. Combine crushed berries with sugar and lemon juice. Simmer gently 5 minutes. Remove from heat and add butter or margarine. Roll scoops of the ice cream in coconut. Place on cookie sheet or shallow dish and return to freezer until ready to serve. To serve: Place coconut balls in serving dishes and top each with a reserved blueberry. Top with the blueberry sauce (either warm or cool).

Yields 6 to 8 servings.

☆ ☆

**If you like *"Recipes of the Stars,"* you'll love
Leo Pearlstein's entertaining book, *"Celebrity Stew:***
*Food Publicity Pioneer Shares 50 Years of Entertaining
Inside Stories of Hollywood Royalty"*
Foreword by Steve Allen

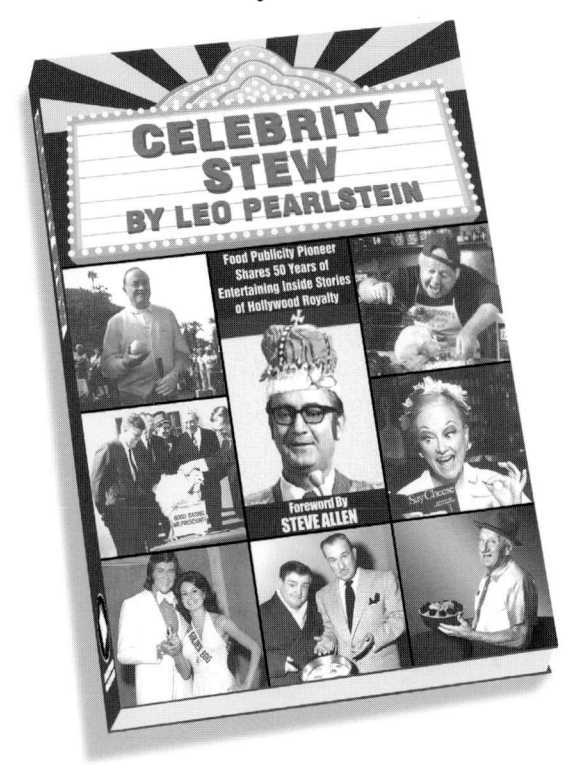

You'll go behind-the-scenes of some of Pearlstein's most zany food publicity activities with many of Hollywood's top celebrities, highlighted by over 200 nostalgic photos.

"'Celebrity Stew' by Leo Pearlstein with a foreword by the late Steve Allen is terrific. After 50 years as the guru of food publicity, you'll hear some juicy celebrity stories that will make your mouth water." **—Larry King, CNN**

"'Celebrity Stew' is a collection of unique and fascinating stories about Hollywood stars and food publicity. Encounters with Bob Hope, Steve Allen, Bing Crosby, Jayne Mansfield, Groucho Marx, Mickey Rooney, Dinah Shore, Phyllis Diller, Abbott & Costello, and a great many more entertainment industry notables are anecdotally detailed in this veritable treasure trove of wit, wisdom, and brushes with celebrity figures. **'Celebrity Stew" is very highly recommended reading,** especially for the legions of fans for radio, film, and television celebrities and stars!" **—Midwest Book Review**

☆ ☆

For information about
Lee & Associates, Inc.
Marketing, Public Relations & Advertising
contact them at:
145 S. Fairfax Ave., Suite 301
Los Angeles, CA 90036
Phone: (323) 938-3300
Email: leeassociatespr@aol.com
Website: www.leeassociates.com